What Industry Experts A

'An essential companion for new managers, blending actionable day-to-day advice with proven methodologies and self-development tools. Clear, practical, and genuinely empowering.'
- Tuca Botelho, Succession Planning Leader, Global Partner, IBM

'Practical, concise, and empowering—this book is a foundational resource for leaders seeking a clear plan and proven strategies for success.'
—Anaf Durrani, Global Chief Technology Officer, Ford Pro, Ford Motor Company

'This book feels like a calm, capable mentor whispering "you've got this" while quietly handing you a colour-coded plan before your first week as a manager derails. It's practical, thoughtfully structured and genuinely supportive without drowning you in buzzwords or ego.'
—Michelle Hartley FCIPD, Founder and MD, People Sorted

'A masterful blend of story telling and simple, actionable frameworks makes this book unforgettable. I would hand it to every new department head in my team as a go-to guide for impactful leadership. It is a must-have leadership crash course!'
—Adnan Kazi, Chief Operating Officer, TenX

'A clear and supportive guide that helps new leaders understand their role, build confidence, and take meaningful action in their first months.'
—Arooj Kalim, Chief Operating Officer, eXectify Personal Branding Solutions

'Loved it! Clear, practical and packed with tools, Whitman's guide is a must-read for new managers seeking confidence and structure.'
—Reedsy

THE ESSENTIAL GUIDE FOR NEW MANAGERS AND TEAM LEADERS

© 2026 by James A. Whitman

First Edition, 2026

ISBN: 978-1-899534-15-9 (paperback)
ISBN: 978-1-899534-13-5 (ebook)

www.oxfordhousemedia.com

Contents

Introduction

Congratulations! Whether you've just stepped into a team leader role, been promoted to a supervisor or a manager, or are thinking about taking the plunge, you've made an exciting choice. Leadership is a journey, and the fact you're here means you're ready to take the first step.

I know how it feels. I've been there. Moving from team member to team leader, then manager, and eventually executive was a steep learning curve. At times, I felt uncertain, overwhelmed, and out of my depth. Experienced leaders were often too busy to guide me. I made mistakes, but I learned a lot. I want to share these lessons with you, so your path is smoother.

This book is your shortcut. It's not about theory or abstract concepts, though I do share useful frameworks. It's about practical, actionable advice you can use every day as a leader and manager.

To make it even more useful, I've included two structured plans:

- **A 30-day plan for new team leaders** to help you build influence, trust, and strong leadership foundations.
- **A 60-day plan for new managers** to help you combine leadership skills with practical management tools like planning, performance, and decision-making.

Why two plans? Team leaders and managers have different roles and responsibilities. Team leaders focus on influence and relationships. Managers balance influence with operational oversight and performance. Each stage requires a different focus, and this book is designed to guide you at the right pace.

Remember Lao Tzu said, 'A journey of a thousand miles begins beneath one's feet'. Take that first step with confidence. This book is your coach, your playbook and your companion. No jargon, no fluff, just guidance you can use.

Let's get started and make this leadership journey a great one.

James A. Whitman

Chapter 1: Understanding the Foundation of Leading People

In 1914, as Ernest Shackleton's ship Endurance became trapped in Antarctic ice, his crew faced months of isolation and bitter cold. One sailor asked, half in despair, *'What does it mean to lead when there's nowhere left to go?'*

Shackleton replied, *'It means making sure no one is lost, not in the ice, and not in spirit.'*

Over two years, he kept every man alive through blizzards, starvation, and hopeless odds. Shackleton never gave grand speeches; he led through calm emphasise, resolve, and shared hardship, proving that true leadership is not about moving forward but about keeping others from falling behind.

Leading people to get things done is as old as humanity. It is such a fundamental aspect of human life that it extends far beyond the realms of business, politics, or the military. Leadership is found in ancient Chinese and Hindu scriptures, in the communal traditions of Indigenous Australians, in the wisdom of some African societies, in the structured civilizations of the Incas, and within religious traditions across the world. The leadership models of Moses and Jesus emphasise servanthood, humility, moral integrity, and care for others, values that stand in stark contrast to authority rooted in power, control, or privilege. Similarly, the Prophet

3

Muhammad advised, *'When three [or more] people set out on a journey, they should appoint one of them as their leader'.*

Defining Leadership and Management

People are often unclear about the disciplines of 'leadership' and 'management', and there's also plenty of debate about what really defines a leader versus a manager. I'll keep it very simple. My view is that while these terms are often used differently depending on context, both are relevant, though they matter in different ways for team leaders and managers.

Defining Leadership

Let's start with a few perspectives on leadership:

'Leadership means making choices and then rallying the team around those choices.' - Satya Nadella (CEO of Microsoft)

'The greatest leader is not necessarily the one who does the greatest things. He is the one that gets the people to do the greatest things.' - Ronald Reagan (40th President of the United States)

*'Only when you can boldly declare, "This is my responsibility",
do you truly become a leader.'* - Konosuke Matsushita (founder of Panasonic)

'Leadership is your instinct, then it's you're training. Leaders are always positive, they never complain.' - Jack Ma (founder of Alibaba)

'In the end, the success of any leader is measured by whether the team is better off because of her leadership.' - Mary Barra (CEO of General Motors)

Leadership is the ability to guide and influence a team towards a shared goal. It's about setting direction, motivating others, building trust, and creating an environment where people can thrive.

At its core, leadership relies on influence rather than authority, combining vision with practical skills. Leaders navigate challenges and help others perform at their best.

In simple terms, leadership is 'making things happen.'

Defining Management

Let's now look at a few perspectives on management:

'Management is doing things right; leadership is doing the right things.' - Peter F. Drucker (Author & Management Consultant)

'Management is efficiency in climbing the ladder of success; leadership determines whether the ladder is leaning against the right wall.' - Stephen R. Covey (Author, The 7 Habits of Highly Effective People)

'Management is about arranging and telling. Leadership is about nurturing and enhancing.' - Tom Peters (Author & Business Management Expert)

Management is the ability to plan, organise, and coordinate resources to achieve specific goals efficiently. It involves allocating tasks and monitoring progress. Setting priorities and ensuring work is completed on time and to standard are also key components of management.

Fundamentally, management relies on three things: structure, processes, and decision-making skills to deliver results. Managers must handle challenges and optimise resources, whilst ensuring the team and organisation stay in order.

In simple terms, management is 'making things work'.

> **Note**: In this book, I often use 'leader' instead of 'manager', 'supervisor' or 'team leader'. If you're guiding even a small group, you are leading and 'leader' fits better.

When to Use These Terms?

Leadership and management play a part at every stage of working life, whether someone is guiding a small team, running a department, or shaping strategy at the top. The balance between the two shifts as responsibilities grow, but each remains essential. Leadership helps set direction and spark motivation, while management keeps day-to-day work organised and moving smoothly. Table 1 shows how the two usually apply in practice.

For example, when a department head leads colleagues through a period of change, leadership becomes central as they share a clear vision and steady the team. Yet, when the same person reviews weekly priorities or coordinates workload, management takes the lead to ensure tasks, timelines, and expectations are handled with care.

Table 1: When to use leadership and management terms.

Leadership	Management
• Mindset and Behaviours	• Performance
• Influencing Others	• Processes and Workflow
• Building Trust	• Planning and Prioritisation
• Motivating Teams	• KPIs, Goals, Metrics
• Culture and Communication	• Decision-Making
• Relationships	• Resource Allocation
• Vision and Purpose	• Accountability
• Emotional Intelligence	• Systems and Tools

In short:

- Leadership is human, relational, and future-focused
- Management is operational, practical, and structure-focused

Challenging the 'Manager' vs. 'Leader' Dichotomy

In 1982, Johnson & Johnson faced a crisis when seven people died from cyanide-laced Tylenol capsules. The product manager acted quickly, overseeing the recall, handling logistics, and leading her teams with calm and strategy. CEO James E. Burke also communicated openly with the public, reinforcing the company's values of safety and trust, and boldly decided to recall 31 million bottles, even before the full risk was clear.

Although their roles differed, both demonstrated these key traits: team guidance, decisive decision making, and motivating people under pressure. Together, they embodied both management and leadership in action.

Yet many writers, academics, and commentators, even those who have never managed people, insist on dividing managers and leaders into neat categories, as if comparing apples to bananas. Managers are often portrayed as practical, task-oriented figures focused solely on execution, while leaders are idealised as visionaries and strategic thinkers, seemingly operating in the clouds with prophetic foresight. Figure 1 from a US university illustrates this simplistic view.

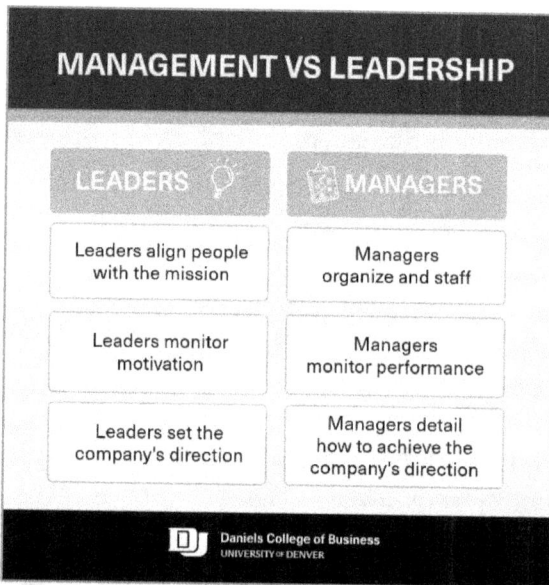

MANAGEMENT VS LEADERSHIP

LEADERS	MANAGERS
Leaders align people with the mission	Managers organize and staff
Leaders monitor motivation	Managers monitor performance
Leaders set the company's direction	Managers detail how to achieve the company's direction

Daniels College of Business
UNIVERSITY OF DENVER

Figure 1: Key differences between leaders and managers according to University of Denver.

Overlapping Roles and Shared Traits

This divide is misleading. Managers and leaders exist on the same continuum, like two ends of the same string, with overlapping traits rather than a sharp divide. The Johnson & Johnson example shows that while their functions and responsibilities differ across organisational layers, the core qualities: vision, motivation, communication, decision-making, and problem-solving, remain consistent. The key distinction lies in the scope of responsibility and accountability, which increases with seniority, as illustrated in Figure 2.

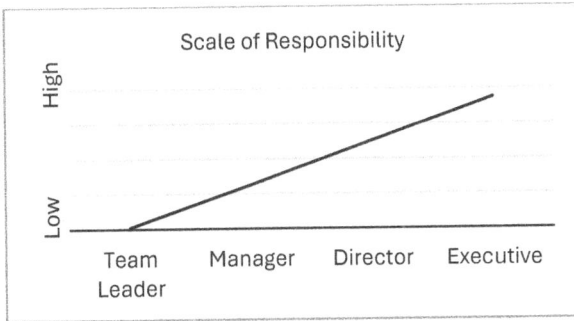

Figure 2: Scale of responsibility across functions.

The simplistic dichotomy presented in Figure 1 fails to reflect this complexity. Figure 3 offers a more accurate representation of the relationship between managers and leaders, highlighting both differences and similarities.

Managers Also Lead, and Leaders Also Manage

My decades of leadership experience have shown me that managers also lead, and leaders also manage. A manager may not hold the same level of responsibility as an executive, but this does not mean they operate mechanically or without vision. Drawing from my own experience as a manager of the Software Division, I led a team of eight salespeople with a $25 million annual target. Success began with setting a clear vision to identify new revenue opportunities and developing a strategic plan to meet those goals. I kept the team focused and adapted to challenges whilst ensuring that we aligned with company objectives.

In addition to strategic planning, I led by example, set the pace, and inspired the team. My responsibilities also included hiring, managing stakeholders, negotiating, and solving problems. Through vision and strategy, I showed that managers don't just manage, they actively *lead* and shape their team's success.

Executives and leaders carry a broader strategic remit, greater responsibility, and oversight of larger budgets. Beyond setting vision and goals, they manage senior teams, provide guidance, motivate staff, make key hiring and firing decisions, and develop top talent. Even at the highest levels, traditional management tasks remain essential.

As mentioned, management and leadership are overlapping roles along a continuum, from team leader all the way to CEO. Tasks and responsibilities expand with seniority, but core traits remain consistent. Team leaders set goals and assert authority. They must make decisions, communicate, motivate, and solve problems. Directors or executives do the same, but on a larger scale, managing entire departments or organisations, as Figure 3 illustrates.

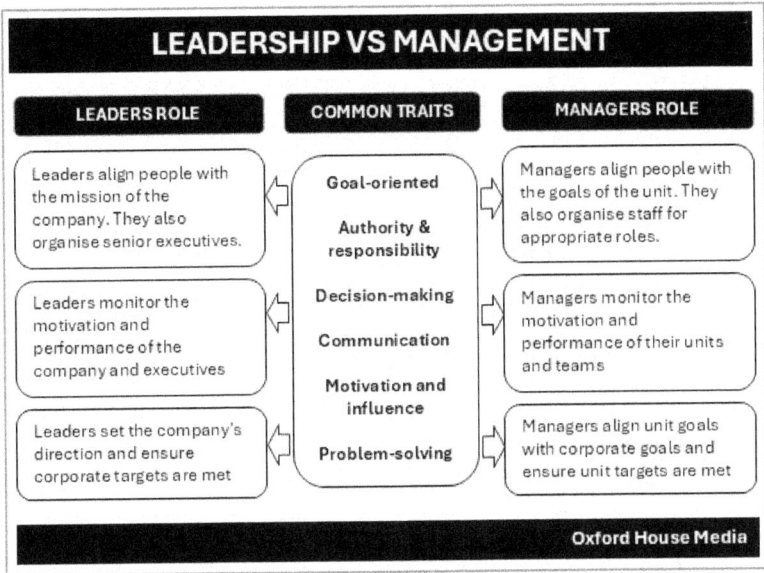

LEADERSHIP VS MANAGEMENT

LEADERS ROLE	COMMON TRAITS	MANAGERS ROLE
Leaders align people with the mission of the company. They also organise senior executives.	Goal-oriented Authority & responsibility	Managers align people with the goals of the unit. They also organise staff for appropriate roles.
Leaders monitor the motivation and performance of the company and executives	Decision-making Communication Motivation and influence	Managers monitor the motivation and performance of their units and teams
Leaders set the company's direction and ensure corporate targets are met	Problem-solving	Managers align unit goals with corporate goals and ensure unit targets are met

Oxford House Media

Figure 3: The role of leaders and managers.

Although function-specific differences exist at higher levels, the similarities outweigh them. At every level, both leaders and managers demonstrate vision, motivation, creativity, and a passion for success.

Words Every New Leader Should Know

As a new leader, you'll come across many words and phrases that are often used in conversations about leadership. It's helpful not only to familiarise yourself with these terms, but also to understand what they truly mean and when to use them. Even more importantly, being able to use them with confidence will show others your sincerity and growing wisdom in your role. Figure 4 illustrates some of these key terms.

Leadership Styles

Definition: Different approaches to leading and managing a team. Common styles include:
- Autocratic
- Democratic
- Transformational
- Laissez-Faire

Importance: Knowing styles enables leaders to adapt their approach to meet the team's needs and the situation.

Emotional Intelligence (EQ)

Definition: The ability to recognise, understand, and manage your emotions and the emotions of others.

Importance: High EQ helps resolve conflicts, build trust, and motivate team members effectively.

Delegation

Definition: Assigning tasks and responsibilities to team members with clear expectations.

Importance: Effective delegation empowers people, improves efficiency, and prevents leader burnout.

Goal Setting

Definition: Creating goals that are clear, trackable, realistic, relevant, and time-bound.

Importance: Helps focus team efforts and ensures clear expectations. Well-defined goals drive performance and align individual work with team objectives.

Feedback (Constructive and Positive)

Definition: Providing timely, specific, and actionable feedback to improve performance and morale.

Importance: Regular feedback helps guide performance, boost engagement, and encourages continuous development.

Conflict Resolution

Definition: The process of resolving disagreements or tensions within the team.

Importance: Effective conflict resolution maintains team harmony, ensures productivity, and reduces stress.

Performance Management

Definition: The process of setting expectations, assessing performance, providing feedback, and supporting employee development.

Importance: It's crucial for tracking progress, addressing issues early, and ensuring the team meets objectives.

Collaboration

Definition: Working together towards a common goal, sharing ideas, resources, and responsibilities.

Importance: Encouraging collaboration helps leverage diverse strengths, fosters creativity, and enhances team performance.

Team Dynamics

Definition: The behavioral patterns and interactions between members of a team.

Importance: Understanding team dynamics helps identify strengths and weaknesses, improves collaboration, and addresses potential conflicts early.

Time Management

Definition: The ability to plan and allocate time effectively for tasks and priorities.

Importance: Essential for meeting deadlines, staying organised, and ensuring team members can balance workload.

Figure 4: Essential leadership vocabulary.

What is 'Value' in Business Context?

It's common to hear people saying, *'We need to deliver more value to our customers'*, *'How are we adding value in this process?'*, and *'We need to focus on high-value activities to drive meaningful results'*.

So 'value' is a word that pops up frequently in workplaces, yet many people don't fully understand what it means. This can be a major problem, because what one person sees as valuable may be completely different from another's perspective, leading to misunderstandings. Let's define it clearly.

Value is the benefit you create for customers, the organisation, or stakeholders, relative to the cost or effort involved.

The 'relative cost' refers to comparing the benefit delivered with the resources spent: time, money, effort or risk. Value exists only when the benefit exceeds the investment.

For example:

- **Customer**: A tool saving 10 hours a week is valuable only if the time saved outweighs £1,000 a month.
- **Business**: A product generating £500,000 revenue but costing £600,000 to launch has negative value.
- **Employee**: Learning a new skill adds little value if 100 hours of training yield minimal performance gain.
- **Shareholder**: An investment is valuable only if the returns exceed the capital and risk involved, increasing long-term growth and profitability.

Understanding Roles and Functions

Western Organisational Roles

As you embark on, or think about, your leadership journey, it's important to look up and ahead to understand the different roles and functions within organisations, because you will be climbing that ladder.

Each role contributes to overall success and knowing how they work together can help you lead more effectively. Table 2 outlines the most common operational roles found in commercial organisations in the West, from team leaders to C-suite executives.

Keep in mind that each organisation may have its own structure and titles, but the core functions generally remain similar. Table 3 shows the non-operational roles and functions.

In non-profit organisations, such as charities and advocacy groups, there are roles not found in the commercial sector. A Programme Manager in a charity might oversee community outreach and fundraising, while roles in advocacy focus on policy analysis and social change. These positions require leadership and an understanding of community needs.

In government, roles like Department Head or Permanent Secretary manage public services such as healthcare and education. Positions like Government Minister in the UK are vital for policy development and implementation. These leaders collaborate with stakeholders and use public relations skills to drive change and meet citizens' needs.

Table 2: Operational roles in Western commercial organisations.

Role	Function (operational)
Team Leader	Oversees a small team. Reports to a supervisor or a manager.
Supervisor	Oversees multiple teams or a larger group, handles day-to-day operations, and reports to managers.
Manager	Manages one or more teams, sets strategy for the team, makes decisions to meet team goals, reports to senior leaders.
General Manager (GM)	Oversees overall operations of a business unit or department.
Director	Oversees a department or functional area, sets strategic direction.
Managing Director (MD) UK / General Manager (GM) US	Senior executive responsible for the day-to-day management of the company or a business unit, often reports directly to the CEO or Board of Directors.
Senior Director	Manages multiple departments or business functions, plays a key role in company strategy, reports to executives.
Vice President (VP)	Leads entire divisions or key functions, part of the executive team, reports to C-suite executives.
Chief Officers (CFO, COO, CTO, CxO etc.)	High-ranking executives responsible for specific functions such as finance (CFO), operations (COO), or technology (CTO).
Chief Executive Officer (CEO)	The highest-ranking executive responsible for the overall success of the company or organisation, making major decisions and setting long-term strategy.

Table 3: Non-operational roles in Western commercial organisations.

Role	Function (non-operational)
Chair / Chairperson	The head of the board of directors, responsible for corporate governance and representing the organisation at the board level. In some US organisations, this role may be split with the CEO.
Board Member / Director	Provides oversight and governance, sets strategic direction with other board members, monitors management performance, and ensures accountability to shareholders, donors, or stakeholders. In non-profits, board members may also oversee compliance, fundraising, and mission alignment.

Global Variations in Organisational Roles

In many non-Western regions, corporate structures and leadership roles often differ from the standard Western model, where authority flows through formal titles. While roles such as 'Chairperson', 'Managing Director', or 'CEO' exist, their actual authority can be shaped by culture, politics, and family influence.

In China, the 'Chairperson' usually outranks the CEO, guiding corporate strategy and maintaining ties with government or Party structures. In South Korea, chaebol conglomerates concentrate power within founding families, where the Chairperson or Vice-Chairman often has more influence than the CEO.

In the Middle East, family-owned businesses see the family head or Chairman as the main decision-maker, with CEOs managing daily operations but ultimately reporting to the family. Similarly, in India and Southeast Asia, formal titles coexist with strong familial or seniority-based influence on decision-making.

Choosing Your Leadership Style

New managers and team leaders rarely have full freedom to choose their leadership style. Your leadership style will mainly depend on where you and your team are located (country or region), company policies, organisational culture, and established norms in the region where you're operating, which influence decision-making, communication, accountability and even hiring.

Having said that, there may well be some room to move as a leadership style is not about rigidly following one model. It involves selecting the approach most likely to work with your team and remaining flexible as circumstances, team readiness, and priorities change. For example, a more directive approach may be needed during periods of change, while a participative style often works best once a team is experienced and settled.

Table 4 provides a quick guide to common leadership styles and the regions where they tend to be most effective. A word of caution: these styles are not set in stone. You may well find that in some regions, such as the Middle East, where there are people from all around the world, a management style might be a blend of several approaches.

Table 4: Typical leadership styles across regions.

Leadership Style	Description
Authoritative (Asia, Middle East, Africa)	Provides clear direction, sets expectations, and makes decisions with a top-down approach. Often used in hierarchical cultures where clarity and control are valued.
Coaching (North America, Europe, Australia)	Focuses on developing team members' skills and potential, providing guidance, mentoring, and ongoing feedback to help individuals grow.
Laissez-Faire (Western Europe, Australia)	Hands-off approach that allows teams high autonomy and self-management. Works best with highly skilled and experienced teams.
Participative (North America, Europe, Latin America)	Involves team members in decision-making, encouraging collaboration and ownership, while still maintaining overall leadership oversight.
Transactional (Global / Multinational)	Emphasises adherence to rules, procedures, and targets, using rewards and penalties to drive performance and ensure task completion.
Transformational (North America, Europe, Africa)	Inspires and motivates teams to embrace change, innovate, and commit to a shared vision, often going beyond short-term goals.

Leading Your Way, No Matter Your Age

You can lead at any age because leadership isn't about how old you are, it's about who you are and what you bring. You can start or pause your leadership journey at any stage of life; there are no strict rules. Some people lead early, others later, and many dip in and out as life changes.

If you've got the confidence, skills and appetite to guide others, you can step into a leadership role and stay there for as long as it suits you. Many commercial organisations follow a typical pattern, as shown in Figure 5, team leader in your 20s, manager in your 30s, senior leader in your 40s, and executive or board roles in your 50s. At what age you lead is not fixed as careers shift, people change direction, and opportunities appear unexpectedly.

Ultimately, leadership is personal. It moves at your pace and on your terms. You choose when to lead and how far to go.

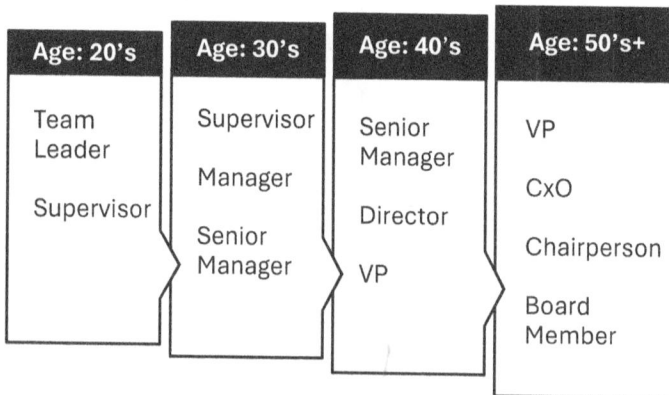

Age: 20's	Age: 30's	Age: 40's	Age: 50's+
Team Leader	Supervisor	Senior Manager	VP
	Manager		CxO
Supervisor	Senior Manager	Director	Chairperson
		VP	Board Member

Figure 5: The typical leadership journey in commercial organisations.

Chapter 2: Establishing Core Values in Leadership Practice

Mary Barra stepped into the role of CEO at General Motors during one of the company's most challenging periods, following the ignition switch recall crisis. It quickly became clear that GM needed more than restructuring; it needed leadership that was accountable and willing to set a new standard. Barra put it plainly:

> *'I'm not asking people to [change]. It's a requirement not only that they hold themselves accountable to do it, but that they hold others accountable.'*

Leadership comes with great responsibility and accountability. Faraz Hasan (Managing Director, TenX, North America) says:

> *'Leadership starts with personal accountability: the buck stops with you. Every action sets the tone and becomes either a positive or negative example for your team.'*

Time and again, successful leaders remind us that credibility and trust are central to effective leadership. Without them, influencing your team and achieving meaningful results becomes incredibly difficult.

Beyond credibility and trust, there are other values every leader should embrace.

As Nadeem Ilyas (Head of Financial Control and Counter Fraud, Department for Transport, UK) says:

> *'Core values define the culture; leadership qualities bring it to life. Together, they create an environment where people trust, collaborate, and deliver their best.'*

His words remind us that leadership isn't just about having the right values written on a wall, rather, it's about demonstrating those values every day through your actions. When values and leadership align, trust grows, collaboration happens naturally, and people genuinely feel able to perform at their best.

These qualities are vital for all leaders, including new team leaders. You can start developing them quickly. Make a strong first impression and build those relationships. Demonstrate your expertise tactfully and understand that integrity earns respect. These actions will help develop collaboration and high performance from the very start.

Let's take a moment to define these key qualities.

Values that guide us:

- Integrity – Doing the right thing, always
- Transparency – Being open and honest in communication
- Credibility – Being believable and dependable
- Trust – Confidence in someone's honesty and reliability
- Respect – Valuing others and their input
- Accountability – Owning actions and results

Leadership and teamwork:

- Empathy – Understanding others' feelings and views
- Communication – Sharing information clearly and effectively
- Collaboration – Working well with others to reach goals
- Feedback – Offering guidance to help others improve
- Delegation – Giving tasks to others while staying responsible
- Conflict Resolution – Settling disagreements fairly

Performance and growth:

- Goal Setting – Defining clear and measurable targets
- Motivation – Inspiring others to do their best
- Adaptability – Adjusting quickly to change
- Continuous Improvement – Always seeking to get better
- Resilience – Bouncing back from setbacks

You must be wondering how do they connect, or which comes first? In Figure 6, a logical order and the relationships between them are shown to help visualise how these concepts interlink.

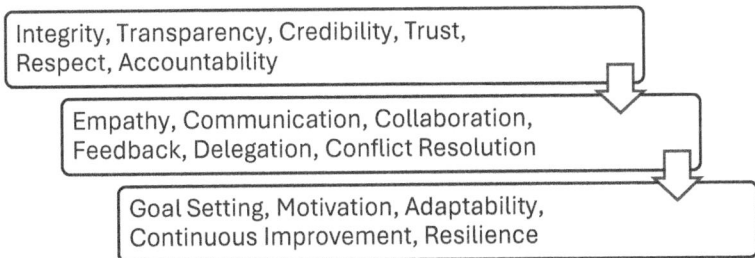

Integrity, Transparency, Credibility, Trust, Respect, Accountability

Empathy, Communication, Collaboration, Feedback, Delegation, Conflict Resolution

Goal Setting, Motivation, Adaptability, Continuous Improvement, Resilience

Figure 6: How core values connect in leadership practice.

First Impressions Matter

Appearance, Behaviour, and Professional Presence

'*You're the best-dressed man in the company*', said one of the account managers to me. I caught myself thinking, '*What a curious thing to say, shouldn't he be talking about revenue instead?*' Once the dust settled, it struck me that first impressions genuinely matter.

During a role in the Middle East, I made a point of having my white cotton shirts and suits professionally laundered and pressed so they stayed perfectly crisp and free of creases. That attention to detail never went unnoticed, it consistently helped me create a strong, positive impression throughout the company.

> "I dress to impress."

The ground reality is that how you present yourself early on sets the tone for your leadership. Dressing appropriately, using positive body language, and speaking with a confident, calm voice all contribute to creating a strong first impression and establishing authority.

As one study notes, managing first impressions can shape how followers perceive a leader's competence and credibility, depending on the context.[1]

---

[1] Al-Shatti, A. (2024) *Does Leaders' Impression Management Help or Hurt? It Depends on the Context.*

24

In another study conducted by Preply, a global online language company, several factors were identified as influencing the formation of first impressions. These are shown in Figure 7.

No.	Factor	Percentage
1	Eye contact and facial expressions	59.5%
2	Personal grooming and hygiene	55.3%
3	Time and punctuality	53.6%
4	Body language and non-verbal cues	53.3%
5	Tone of voice and communication style	53.1%
6	Level of professionalism and preparedness	44.7%
7	Clothing and attire	41.6%
8	Level of confidence and assertiveness	41.1%
9	Physical appearance	39.8%
10	Previous interactions or reputation	21.7%
11	Surrounding environment	11.3%

Figure 7: The percentage of each factor influencing first impression according to Preply.

Projecting Confidence without Arrogance

Confidence is crucial but avoid crossing into arrogance; in other words, don't have an inflated sense of self-importance that leads you to dismiss others' opinions, overestimate your abilities, and act entitled or superior.

New managers must quickly develop the skill of building strong relationships. Being approachable is essential as it leads to respect and trust. Approachability in a leadership style shows that you are empathetic and accessible, rather than distant or authoritarian.

Being Authentic and Genuine

Avoid a 'Walmart smile,' as it can backfire. Smiles in retail are often part of corporate expectations rather than a natural expression. In busy environments with long shifts and demanding customers, maintaining a constant pleasant expression can seem forced, which is why such smiles are sometimes perceived as fake.

Authenticity builds trust, and it comes from being the 'real you'. Show your true self, be honest in your interactions, and avoid pretending to know everything. When your team sees you as genuine, they are more likely to engage and respect your leadership.

> **Tip:** Ways to demonstrate authenticity
>
> - Admit what you don't know and be willing to learn
> - Share your thinking when making decisions
> - Be consistent in your words and actions
> - Listen actively and respond honestly to feedback

Demonstrating Competence

Demonstrating Your Expertise

Consistently meeting deadlines, producing high-quality work, and following through on promises and commitments earns respect and reinforces your competence. Share your subject-matter knowledge when appropriate to show your expertise but avoid micromanaging; empower your team to make their own decisions. Showing expertise reinforces competence, and people are less likely to take you for a ride.

Personally, I prefer not to tell people what to do in areas where I have some expertise, such as selling. I usually share my expertise through questions. For example, if a deal is stalling despite my salesperson having done everything they could, I would not say, *'Go and do this and that'*. Instead, I would ask thoughtful questions such as:

> *'How did you verify that the solution/product meet the customer's requirements?'*

> *'Do you have a relationship with the decision-maker?'*

> *'Does the customer have an approved budget for this year?'*

> *'Who are we competing with?'*

This approach demonstrates my deep expertise while prompting the salesperson to think critically and revisit these areas. It creates a valuable learning opportunity without micromanaging.

Integrity and Consistency

Following Through on Commitments

In his book *Selling in the Middle East*, Shabir Ahmad says:

'During my team leader days, I once asked my line manager to re-evaluate my salary package after a promotion. He told me to remind him at my next appraisal. I did but he then responded, "My policy is to evaluate at year end only." This man was not honest and played with words to stall my request. It destroyed my confidence in him and made me start looking for a way out of his team. I must admit, I was quietly delighted when he was let go just six months later!'

Integrity is earned through consistency. Keep your promises, meet deadlines, and follow through on your commitments.

> *"I don't promise what I won't deliver."*

When your team sees that you can be trusted, they are more likely to invest their efforts in working with you. On the other hand, failing to follow through destroys trust.

Aligning Actions with Values

Your behaviour as a leader should align closely with the values you promote. Make decisions that reflect your company's core values and demonstrate transparency in your reasoning. When your actions match your words, your credibility grows stronger.

Never make the mistake of publicly criticising corporate values or goals when you are in a leadership role. Disagreements are inevitable, but these must be discussed in a one-to-one meeting with your line manager or someone above. If you are seen to deviate from the company's values, your teams will respond accordingly, and you risk losing influence over them. Yes, as a leader, you must 'toe the line'.

Research supports that the greater the consistency between a leader's observed behaviour and followers' expectations, the stronger the level of trust in that manager.[2] When leaders live the values they espouse, employee trust, engagement, and credibility rise significantly.

Transparency and Honesty

Building Trust Through Clear Communication

George Bernard Shaw (playwright, critic, essayist and political activist, Ireland) once remarked, *'The single biggest problem in communication is the illusion that it has taken place.'* His words capture a truth that every leader should remember. Trust begins with clarity. When decisions are

"Truth may burn, but I hold it firm."

made, take the time to explain the reasons behind them. Clear and transparent communication doesn't just share information; it strengthens confidence in your leadership and builds a base for genuine trust. In fact, research shows that transparent communication combined with transformational leadership boosts organisational trust and encourages employee openness to change.[3]

---

[2] J. Dirks and D. Ferrin, 'The Role of Trust in Organisational Settings', *Organization Science*, 12(4), 450–467.

[3] Zainab, B., Akbar, W. & Siddiqui, F. 2021. 'Impact of transformational leadership and transparent communication on employee openness to change: mediating role of employee-organisation trust and moderated role of change-related self-efficacy'. *Leadership & Organisation Development Journal* 43(1), 1–13.

Explaining the Rationale Behind Choices

Whenever you make a decision that affects the team, take the time to explain your thought process, not just what the decision is, but why it was made. Providing that context allows the team to see the bigger picture. It reduces uncertainty and ensures everyone is aligned with organisational goals. People are far more likely to support a decision or change request when they understand the 'why' as it helps them feel informed and part of the process. Be careful, there may be confidential matters that cannot be shared, but my experience shows that majority of management decisions don't fall in this category.

In fact, recent research supports this. In a survey of 73 companies, 74.6% said that performance clearly improved when there was transparency in decision-making, while more than half identified alignment, accountability, and employee engagement as direct benefits of sharing the rationale behind decisions.

Encouraging Open Dialogue

Encourage your team to ask questions and voice concerns. Open dialogue promotes inclusivity and ensures decisions are understood and considered from multiple perspectives.

However, be mindful when managing international teams. In some cultures, such as India and parts of the Middle East, team members may be reluctant to challenge their superiors directly. In Japan, open discussion where dissenting views are expressed in a group setting is generally not acceptable.

Instead, people typically share their differences afterwards in one-to-one sessions.

For further guidance on managing international teams, refer to Chapter 7.

Being Consistent with Messaging

Being consistent with your messaging reinforces your leadership's reliability. Research shows that each 5% increase in the proportion of team members reporting a high level of teamwork was associated with a 7% lower chance of staff perceiving inconsistent communication.[4]

So, when you communicate key decisions or changes, ensure your message is clear, coherent and aligned across all channels. This reduces uncertainty and helps your team understand what the organisation stands for and where it's heading.

If your messaging is inconsistent, people may perceive you as dishonest or incompetent, which will erode your credibility.

Transparency and Honesty Drive Success

Honesty is at the heart of good leadership, but its impact goes beyond simply managing a team.

In sales, a leader who is open about pricing, product limitations, or market conditions helps their team speak confidently with clients, building trust and avoiding misunderstandings. In customer service, being upfront about delays, mistakes, or

---

[4] https://pmc.ncbi.nlm.nih.gov/articles/PMC7024626

policy changes gives staff the tools to solve problems quickly while keeping customers satisfied. In client relationships, leaders who share the full picture, even when things aren't perfect, create reliability and respect that money can't buy.

Transparency also shapes how decisions are made. When a company rolls out a new strategy, leaders who explain why, what the expected outcomes are, and what challenges might arise make it easier for everyone to get on board. Hiding information, on the other hand, breeds confusion and frustration. Leaders who prioritise honesty and openness don't just get better results from stronger team performance to happier clients; they earn genuine respect and trust.

Case Study: Transparency and honesty lead to more revenue

An individual successfully sold software worth over a million dollars to a major bank. The implementation services were offered separately from the software acquisition. When the client sought an honest opinion about the company's implementation services, the individual candidly stated that a competitor provided better services, although his own company was also capable of delivering the job.

This honesty did not lead to a loss of business. Instead, it strengthened the relationship with the bank. Impressed by the company's transparency, the bank decided to proceed with their services, confident in their commitment to deliver due to their demonstrated integrity.

Source: Ahmad, S. (2025). *Selling in the Middle East*. Oxford House Media.

Sharing Both Good and Bad News

Being transparent isn't just about celebrating wins; it's also about being honest when things go wrong. I once managed clustered servers for NatWest, a major bank in the UK. When a new system went live, we accidentally mismatched server memory, causing performance issues that could have disrupted critical operations. We spotted and fixed it quickly, but my manager didn't want to admit it had been our mistake, worried we might jeopardise the contract. I couldn't lie, so when the client investigated, I told them the truth. It was nerve-wracking, but they appreciated our honesty, even thanked us for being upfront and we kept the contract.

Remember, life is never perfect, and delays or missed deadlines are part of life, and people can tolerate these if they are informed upfront.

Being Optimistic

I'm always optimistic. Optimism is a key trait that leaders must have, as it benefits everyone and there is plenty of research to back this.

Martin Seligman (Director, Positive Psychology Centre, University of Pennsylvania, USA) found that optimists enjoy better health, perform more effectively, *"Optimism is woven in my DNA."* achieve greater success, and experience less stress. For example, a 35-year study of Harvard students found that those optimistic at age 25 were significantly healthier at 45 and 60 than their pessimistic peers.[5]

More recent research in China also strongly supports optimism in the workplace.[6] A 2023 study of 653 nurses across hospitals found that optimism positively influences job performance and wellbeing, particularly when combined with perceived organisational support, and it has positive impact on managing stress.

Optimistic individuals perform better, and they are better equipped to handle setbacks and often turn challenges into opportunities, maintaining hope and resilience in the face of adversity. You must learn to become optimistic; it's a vital component in your leadership toolbox.

So, how do you become optimistic? This is a million-dollar question. Here is my take on this:

- **Look for the silver lining**: When things go wrong, try to see what can be learned or what opportunities might come from it, rather than focusing on the setback.
- **Keep a gratitude habit**: Take time each day to notice and appreciate the good things in your life, however small, they help shift your focus from what's missing to what's working.

---

[5] Waldinger, R. and Schulz, M., 2023. The Good Life: Lessons from the World's Longest Scientific Study of Happiness. New York: Simon & Schuster.
[6] Li, X., Zhang, Y., & Wang, H., 'Perceived organisational support for strengths use and its impact on nurses' job performance: The mediating roles of control beliefs about stress and optimism', *PubMed*, 2023, https://pubmed.ncbi.nlm.nih.gov/39046241/

- **Choose your company wisely:** Spend time with positive, supportive people and engage with uplifting stories or communities; they naturally lift your outlook.

The last point above is very important in my eyes. Always surround yourself with positive, uplifting people. A parable that illustrates this is:

> *'The example of a good companion and a bad companion is like that of a perfume-seller and a blacksmith. The perfume-seller may give you fragrance, or at the very least enjoy a pleasant smell. As for the blacksmith, he may scorch your clothes, or you may inhale an unpleasant smell.'*

Choosing the right company can subtly shape your outlook, just as a gentle fragrance lifts the spirit while a harmful influence can weigh it down.

Chapter 3: A New Leader Integration Plan

In his youth in Philadelphia, Benjamin Franklin (Founding Father, USA), committed himself to thirteen personal virtues, including order and industry. He carefully planned his days in a small notebook, setting aside time for reading, work, and reflection. Whenever he drifted from this routine, his productivity suffered, teaching him that even the strongest intentions can falter without a clear plan.

His familiar line, *'If you fail to plan, you are planning to fail'*, captures his belief that preparation, not luck, drives success.

The same applies to leadership. The first 30 to 60 days in a new role are critical for team leaders and managers, while executives may need closer to 90. These early weeks shape how your team sees you, influence how goals are met, and build your credibility. From experience, a clear, structured roadmap is essential; a framework I call the 'New Leader Integration Plan.'

The following high-level plan outlines are about building relationships with the team, prioritising department or unit goals and delivering useful results early.

30-Day Plan: For new team leaders to begin to build trust, understand the team dynamics, and achieve early results.

60-Day Plan: For new supervisors and managers to align teams, optimise processes, and strengthen performance.

Executives often require a 90-day integration period, though the executive plan is outside the scope of this book.

The focus of the first 30-day and 60-day can be broadly categorised into three areas:

1) **Getting to know your team and key stakeholders:** This area focuses on understanding your team by observing interactions and building relationships, in addition to identifying key internal and external stakeholders.

2) **Setting direction and establishing early results:** This area is about translating insights from the first category into clear plans by aligning with organisational priorities and goals and creating early momentum.

3) **Driving team performance and continuous growth:** This area emphasises active leadership through performance management, coaching, communication, accountability, and long-term team and personal development.

Subsequent chapters, after the 30- and 60-day plans, explore these areas in more detail. They aren't in strict order, but each concept links to your tasks. You can revisit chapters as needed, apply practical strategies, and focus on what's most relevant. The goal is to help you tackle your task list with confidence and grow into your role as a leader in a realistic, hands-on way.

A 30-Day Plan for New Team Leaders

Goal: To build trust, understand the team, and establish a solid leadership base.

- **Week 1 – Observe and Understand**
  You should concentrate on listening and learning how the team works, noting workflows, roles, and informal dynamics while avoiding quick changes.

- **Week 2 – Build Relationships and Trust**
  Focus moves to forming genuine connections through empathy, one-to-ones, clear expectations, and open communication.

- **Week 3 – Set Direction and Priorities**
  You sharpen priorities, aligns tasks with wider goals, delegates to strengths, and encourages collaborative improvements.

- **Week 4 – Take Ownership and Establish Routines**
  You establish routines, reviews progress, offers clear feedback, recognises achievements, and reflects on effectiveness.

Key outcome: Your team gets to know you, trusts you, gets a feel for your leadership style, and starts working together more smoothly.

A 30-Day Team Leaders Checklist

Week 1	Observe and Understand	(✓)
	Meet with each team member	☐
	Monitor team interactions	☐
	Understand unwritten rules	☐
	Review key documents	☐
	Meet with senior leaders	☐
	Expand your people network	☐
	Identify key stakeholders	☐
	Prioritise listening and observation	☐

Week 2	Build Relationships and Trust	(✓)
	Schedule one-on-one check-ins	☐
	Show interest in team members' goals	☐
	Communicate expectations clearly	☐
	Identify early wins for the team	☐

Week 3	Set Direction and Priorities	(✓)
	Clarify team objectives and alignment	☐
	Delegate tasks based on strengths	☐
	Encourage feedback and collaboration	☐
	Introduce small process improvements	☐

Week 4	Take Ownership and Establish Routines	(✓)
	Hold team meeting to review progress	☐
	Provide constructive feedback	☐
	Recognise achievements	☐
	Establish regular team routines	☐
	Reflect on leadership style	☐

A 60-Day Plan for Supervisors and Managers

Goal: To move from daily oversight to guiding how the team operates and contributes to wider goals.

- **Weeks 1 to 2 – Understand and Assess**
  In the first fortnight, you listen, observe, meet key people, reviews core data, and note team culture to build clarity before acting.

- **Weeks 3 to 4 – Align and Plan**
  After gathering insights, set clear objectives, assign responsibilities, communicate expectations, and implement small improvements to drive results.

- **Weeks 5 to 6 – Lead and Develop**
  You should emphasise coaching, skill development, feedback, collaboration, and effective resource use to meet priorities.

- **Weeks 7 to 8 – Monitor and Optimise**
  The final fortnight focuses on tracking progress, adjusting plans, recognising successes, addressing challenges, and refining leadership for greater effectiveness.

> **Key outcome:** The team knows goals, processes run smoothly, progress is tracked, and your leadership and operations are balanced.

A 60-Day Supervisors and Managers Checklist

	Observe and Understand	(✓)
Weeks 1–2	Meet with each team member and key stakeholders	☐
	Monitor team interactions and collaboration	☐
	Understand unwritten rules, culture and team dynamics	☐
	Review processes, workflows, and key documents	☐
	Meet with senior leaders to confirm expectations	☐
	Map and expand your internal network	☐
	Identify early quick wins and priority areas	☐
	Prioritise listening and observation	☐

	Build Relationships and Align	(✓)
Weeks 3–4	Schedule one-on-one check-ins to build trust	☐
	Show interest in team members' goals and strengths	☐
	Communicate expectations clearly and consistently	☐
	Clarify team objectives and alignment with organisation goals	☐
	Begin assigning responsibilities based on strengths	☐
	Introduce small process improvements	☐
	Encourage open feedback and collaboration	☐

	Set Direction, Lead and Develop	(✓)
Weeks 5–6	Provide coaching and support based on needs	☐
	Hold performance and development conversations	☐
	Delegate effectively and empower team members	☐
	Encourage innovation, ownership, and problem-solving	☐
	Ensure resources match priorities and workload	☐
	Strengthen team routines and communication	☐

	Take Ownership, Monitor and Optimise	(✓)
Weeks 7–8	Track progress against KPIs and team goals	☐
	Adjust plans based on results and team feedback	☐
	Hold team meeting to review progress and next steps	☐
	Recognise achievements and address challenges quickly	☐
	Provide ongoing constructive feedback	☐
	Reflect on and refine your leadership style	☐
	Review team capacity and make decisions on hiring, support, or performance	☐

Chapter 4: Getting to Know Your Team and Key Stakeholders

One-to-One Sessions with Team Members

Getting to know your team is one of the first and most critical steps, after all, you have been hired to lead or manage this team. It's your key responsibility!

Taking the time to understand each team member's strengths, challenges, and career aspirations helps to build rapport and trust. Personal conversations allow people to open as it demonstrates your genuine interest in their well-being and development.

I don't rely on an official two-day team-building retreat to connect with my team. Instead, I meet team members for coffee or lunch, stay quiet, and genuinely listen; two ears, one mouth. I often schedule 30 to 60-minute one-on-one chats in a quiet space, which also provides a perfect opportunity to jot down key observations and details about each person. Listening always works.

For those new to managing people, using structured frameworks to capture strengths and weaknesses during these meetings can make understanding your team much easier.

Recognising Team Strengths and Weaknesses

A a good leader, you should recognise both the strengths and areas for development within their team. Here are a few frameworks you can use to help.

One widely used framework for recording team members' strengths and weaknesses is the Strengths, Weaknesses, Opportunities and Threats (SWOT) analysis, adapted for individuals rather than organisations.

Figure 8 shows an example for a team member called Amelia, who manages customers at a retail outlet. You don't need tools to create wonderful graphics; I just draw this on a piece of paper if I am short of time. The point is to just capture the information.

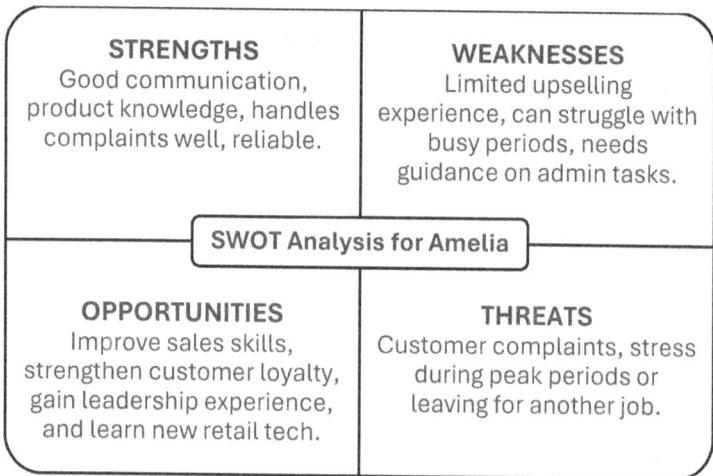

STRENGTHS	WEAKNESSES
Good communication, product knowledge, handles complaints well, reliable.	Limited upselling experience, can struggle with busy periods, needs guidance on admin tasks.

SWOT Analysis for Amelia

OPPORTUNITIES	THREATS
Improve sales skills, strengthen customer loyalty, gain leadership experience, and learn new retail tech.	Customer complaints, stress during peak periods or leaving for another job.

Figure 8: Team SWOT Analysis.

Other frameworks that can complement or replace SWOT include:

- **360-Degree Feedback:** Collects input from peers, managers, and subordinates to give a rounded view of strengths and weaknesses.
- **Performance Appraisal Matrix:** Rates team members across key competencies, with clear areas for improvement and development goals.
- **Competency Framework:** Lists required skills for roles and tracks which team members meet, exceed, or need development in each competency.
- **Talent Grid (9-Box Matrix):** Plots performance against potential, helping identify high performers, emerging talent, and areas needing support.

For practical use, a combination of a Competency Framework with 360-Degree Feedback often gives the most useful insight, as it records both observable performance and developmental needs without being overly subjective.

A list of key frameworks that managers may find useful can be found in Appendix A.

Monitor Team Interactions

When you join a team, take a bit of time to watch how people interact. Understanding how the group communicates and works together will help you spot any issues early, make the most of everyone's strengths, and build a team that really works well together.

At this beginning stage, observation is key, not fixes. Don't rush into changing anything without getting to know the people and processes. A previous manager taught me a valuable lesson: when managing a new team, don't fix what isn't broken. We

> "I don't fix what's not broken."

had regular weekly online meetings, and he didn't change them. For the first month, he simply listened. He maintained the format, then gradually adapted the meetings to fill gaps he noticed. By doing this, he didn't disrupt a process that already worked, and the team welcomed the improvements without resistance.

Understand Unwritten Rules

Good leaders know the value of listening and observing before acting. Girish Mathrubootham (CEO & Founder, Freshworks, India) puts humans first, emphasising that trust comes from *'earning trust through a heart-led approach... [by] doing the right thing by them'*. Fred Swaniker (founder, African Leadership Academy, Ghana) learned that humility is key, *'Leaders talk less and speak last. First listen. We are as important as other people are.'*

In South America, a CEO of a major healthcare provider established credibility by engaging informally and adapting to local communication and hierarchy. These leaders show that understanding unwritten rules is key to building trust.

> **Lesson**: Every team has unspoken rules. Listening and observing help you understand their communication and preferences.

Review Key Documents

'Do not test the depth of the river with both feet'. This African proverb reminds us to proceed carefully and understand the situation before fully committing. Similarly, when starting your first role as a new manager or team leader, reviewing the right company documents allows you to quickly grasp your responsibilities, get to know your team, and understand the organisation. Taking this cautious, informed approach gives you a strong foothold early on.

The first step is to revisit your job description and memorise it. That's a logical starting point. From there, you can start exploring and filling in the knowledge gaps around you. Key documents to focus on are listed below, though not in any order. You may not be able to access all of them. That is fine, focus on doing your best with what is available. In time, you will acquire the missing information.

- **Roles**: Know your responsibilities; clarify team members' roles through discussion if no formal docs exist.
- **Team and performance plans**: Check charters, KPIs, dashboards, and past reviews to see how success is measured.
- **Policies and procedures**: Follow HR, compliance, and operational guidelines; usually on intranet or shared drives.
- **Budget and finance**: Understand team and project budgets, costs, and revenue targets.

- **Project documentation**: Learn from completed reports and lessons learned; note gaps where failures weren't recorded.
- **Company updates**: Stay current with newsletters, announcements, and town hall summaries.
- **Training and onboarding**: Make use of these guides to understand processes and expectations, check HR or line management if unavailable.
- **Organisational charts**: Identify key people and decision-making structures; organisational charts are easy to find.
- **Vision and strategy**: Review vision and strategic plans to understand priorities.

Meet with Senior Leaders

It is vital that you quickly identify who the 'movers and shakers' are in your organisation, who depends on you, and, most importantly, who you will depend on as part of your role. This requires you to meet many people, especially the senior leaders in the company.

Purpose of these meetings are to:

- Understand their priorities and expectations, and how they define success.
- Clarify how your team's work aligns with wider organisational goals.
- Identify opportunities for collaboration and support.

- Build relationships and credibility early on, showing that you are proactive and engaged.
- Give you visibility and importance. They should know you, otherwise the old saying might become true, 'out of sight, out of mind'.

People are generally happy when they feel valued, and leaders appreciate being seen as reference points. By meeting with them, you are, in effect, acknowledging their importance. It's a natural human trait; many people like to feel a little 'pampered' or receive some attention. Leaders thrive when they feel recognised and building that connection not only strengthens your relationship with them but also shows you understand the value of people at all levels.

Expand Your People Network

When Reid Hoffman was building LinkedIn in the early 2000s, he didn't just rely on his technical skills or knowledge of the tech industry. He actively leveraged his network, connecting with classmates, colleagues, and key figures in Silicon Valley. These relationships helped him secure early funding and recruit top talent. He gained strategic advice that was vital to LinkedIn's launch and growth.

Hoffman himself has said that building the right network, knowing the right people, was as important as any business plan or technical insight. In his book *The Start-up of You* (co-authored with Ben Casnocha), Hoffman writes, '*Your network is your net worth. In today's world, your peers and network are often more important than your boss...*'

In one podcast episode linked to the book he says, *'If you're an elite professional ... you can probably find another amazing job by Monday ... just from people in your network.'*

The lesson here is clear: look for opportunities to connect with people. You can start with internal organisational chart if you are new to the company, and there's no better excuse than to walk over and introduce yourself.

If you've been promoted within your existing company, make sure to reach out to the senior leaders. Your excuse could be that you want to learn more about what they do!

> **Takeaway:** Your peers and network are often more important than your boss!

Identify People of Importance

'It's not what you know, but who you know' is a timeless truth in business. Simply meeting senior people or growing your network isn't enough. You need to understand who the important people are, as they'll have a major influence on your working life; they are known as the stakeholders. These are the individuals who can help shape your career and provide valuable opportunities. It's essential to know their priorities and win their support. You should align your efforts with their goals to ensure mutual success and progress.

A good leader develops the skills of a seasoned politician, someone who knows how to bring people on their side and create positive relationships. *'Bringing everyone on the journey is vital for success,*' says Majad Hussain, a digital transformation project manager. It's important to focus on building those connections and really understanding what drives your stakeholders. This will be key to your leadership, helping you tackle challenges and make the most of opportunities when they come your way.

Who is a Stakeholder?

Stakeholders are anyone who has an interest in, influence over, or is affected by your team's work. Real examples include:

- **Internal senior leaders**: Your manager, directors, or executives who set priorities and evaluate performance.
- **Team members**: Those who report to you or work alongside you, directly impacted by your decisions.
- **Other departments**: Colleagues in finance, HR, IT, or operations who collaborate with your team or rely on its outputs.
- **Clients or customers:** Internal or external customers who use your team's services or products.
- **Suppliers or vendors**: External organisations providing goods or services your team depends on.
- **Regulatory bodies**: These are agencies or authorities that establish compliance requirements relevant to your team's work.
- **Project sponsors**: Individuals who fund or champion initiatives your team is responsible for delivering.

Steps to Identify Stakeholders

How do you get to know the stakeholders? You might find this in project documentation, but in other areas, there probably won't be anything documented. You'll need to build this map. How do you do build your own stakeholder map? Figure 9 shows steps to identify stakeholders.

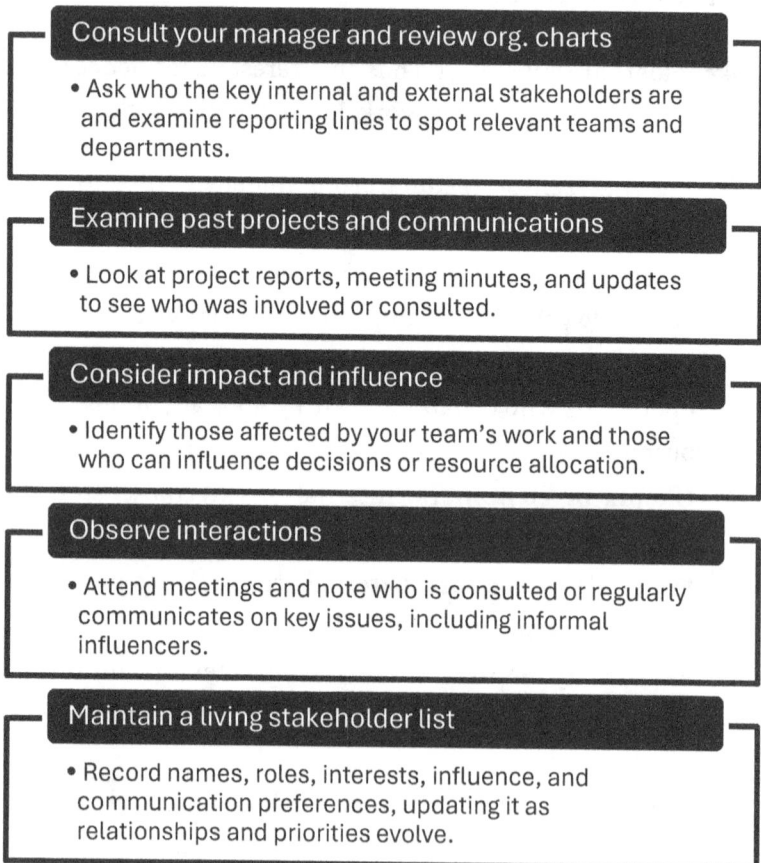

Consult your manager and review org. charts
- Ask who the key internal and external stakeholders are and examine reporting lines to spot relevant teams and departments.

Examine past projects and communications
- Look at project reports, meeting minutes, and updates to see who was involved or consulted.

Consider impact and influence
- Identify those affected by your team's work and those who can influence decisions or resource allocation.

Observe interactions
- Attend meetings and note who is consulted or regularly communicates on key issues, including informal influencers.

Maintain a living stakeholder list
- Record names, roles, interests, influence, and communication preferences, updating it as relationships and priorities evolve.

Figure 9: Steps to identify stakeholders.

Prioritise Listening and Observation

When Anne M. Mulcahy (former chair and CEO of Xerox, USA) took the helm in 2001, the company faced near-collapse with heavy debt and regulatory investigations. Morale was undoubtedly at an all-time low. She launched a listening tour which meant she visited major offices, talked candidly with employees and customers, acknowledged problems, and invoked a shared mission to turn things around.

Her approach was direct: *'If you schmooze and spin your communications, it comes back to bite you in your ability to establish credibility'*, she later reflected. By leading with authenticity and transparency she quickly earned the workforce's trust. Within a few years, Xerox regained profitability and restored its reputation.

Your first actions, like Mulcahy's, matter: be reliable, fair, competent, communicate clearly, keep promises, and show respect. Early demonstration of these behaviours earns peoples respect and trust which, crucially, lays the foundation for long-term success.

Asking Purposeful Questions

When Emma was promoted to project lead at a fast-growing tech firm, she thought she was doing everything right. In meetings, she often found herself checking emails or thinking about what to say next while her team spoke. One day, after a tense discussion, a colleague gently told her, *'Emma, it feels like you're not really hearing me.'*

That hit home. She must avoid multitasking, should'nt interrupt, and listen to understand. From that moment, Emma made a conscious effort to be fully present. She stopped planning her responses mid-conversation and asked questions to really understand what her team was saying.

The change was immediate. Team members engagement improved, and solutions came more quickly because everyone felt understood. Being a leader is not about having all the answers; it's about listening deeply enough to uncover them.

Active listening is just as important as speaking clearly. Ask open-ended questions and encourage honest discussion. You should show that you genuinely value your team's perspective. When you listen with intent, you create a stronger, more collaborative team.

> **Lesson:** Both real-world observations and research show that listening without distractions builds trust and improves communication.

Reflecting and Confirming Understanding

To demonstrate that you're truly listening, reflect what you've heard by paraphrasing or summarising key points. This shows your team that you're engaged and that their opinions matter. Confirming understanding also helps to avoid misunderstandings and ensures that everyone is on the same page.

CHAPTER 5: SETTING DIRECTION AND ESTABLISHING EARLY WINS

Chapter 5: Setting Direction and Establishing Early Wins

Aligning with Organisational Objectives

To lead effectively as a new manager or a team leader, you need to understand your department's or unit's direction, priorities, and goals. It directly supports the organisation's success when your team's work aligns with these objectives.

If you are a new team leader, you may not be expected to connect your team's work to the organisation's broader vision, mission, strategy or goals right away. These are usually broken down into layers for different levels of the organisation, and your line manager or unit head can guide you in understanding them and show you where your team fits in the big picture.

However, you will encounter the words vision, mission and strategy and KPIs everywhere, from organisations public financial reports to internal memos, but don't panic. Here's a quick overview of what they mean:

- **Vision**: A forward-looking statement outlining the organisation's desired future. Simply put, it is what we aim to achieve. Example: Engro Corporation (Pakistan): 'To be the leading investor and wealth-creator of value-driven businesses.'
- **Mission**: The organisation's core purpose guiding its actions. Simply put, it is how we plan to achieve our

vision. Example: Toyota (Japan): 'Producing Happiness for All.'

- **Strategy:** The approach used to achieve vision and mission. Simply put, it is how we will get there. Example: Tesco focuses on operational efficiency, digital innovation, and customer engagement through its Clubcard loyalty scheme to support growth.
- **KPI / Goal:** A measurable value to track success. Simply put, it is how we measure progress. Example: Amazon (USA) stated that it tracks customer and revenue growth, repeat purchases, and brand strength in its 2024 Annual Report.

Setting Clear Goals and Prioritisation

Julia Stewart (former CEO of IHOP and founder of Alurx, USA) exemplifies the power of clear goal setting and prioritisation. She attributes her success to a lifelong habit of writing down her goals. From her school days, she maintained a visible list that covered her career, family, and community priorities. Stewart believes that writing down a goal creates accountability, ensuring focus and progress. As she puts it, *'you can't hit a target you can't see'*, emphasising the importance of clarity. Her disciplined approach provided direction and consistency.

Effective leaders can take a leaf out of her book. Prioritising time and energy ensure that both they and their teams focus on what truly matters. Setting clear goals drives productivity and avoids confusion. It requires understanding the bigger picture, breaking down organisational objectives into simpler tasks, and creating a structured plan to manage time and priorities.

Supporting data further shows the importance of setting clear goals. Research by Dominique Morisano, in her paper *Setting, Elaborating, and Reflecting on Personal Goals Improves Academic Performance*, found that students who set specific and clear goals were better able to focus on what truly matters and avoid distractions. This principle can be

> *"I can't hit a target I can't see."*

applied in the workplace, improving resource allocation and overall efficiency. Similarly, other studies that show that entrepreneurs who set clear business goals tend to have greater long-term success.

Table 5 illustrates the importance of setting goals and recognising the achievements of teams.

Table 5: Setting clear goals leads to improvements.

Employees who set goals are 14.2 times more likely to feel inspired at work.	Employees with clearly defined goals are also 3.6 times more likely to stay committed to their organisation.
Goal setting also increases job satisfaction, with employees being 6.7 times more likely to feel proud of their organisation.	Employees with clear goals are 8.1 times more likely to actively seek ways to improve their work.

Source: BI WORLDWIDE

Managing Time and Tasks

Good planning goes hand in hand with managing your time well and knowing what to prioritise. Being able to push back on non-critical requests is equally important, as it frees you to concentrate on what truly matters. As Steve Jobs once put it, *'Focus is about saying no'*.

Daily Routines for Time Management

Sheryl Sandberg (COO, Meta, USA) demonstrates disciplined time management. She blocks mornings for strategic thinking, holds regular one-to-ones, and plans tasks in advance to avoid being overwhelmed by emails or interruptions. This keeps her organised and focused, supporting her team and priorities.

Elon Musk (CEO, Tesla & SpaceX, USA) also follows a structured schedule, breaking his day into five-minute blocks, prioritising key tasks, delegating, and regularly reviewing progress to use time efficiently.

These examples show that successful leaders structure routines not just to manage work, but to make time for strategic thinking and team development. You don't need expensive apps; Outlook Calendar works well or stick with paper and pen if that suits you!

The point above is about tools, but project management remains essential. Strong project management helps leaders prioritise tasks, optimise resources, and track progress, enabling more effective guidance. As you advance in leadership, these skills will become more valuable and worth developing.

If you are struggling to manage time and prioritising tasks, a time management matrix (or Eisenhower Matrix), as shown in Figure 10, may help. To use it, you need to organise your tasks into four categories:

- **Urgent and important**: Tackle these first. Items with closer deadlines and greater impact should be prioritised at the top of your list.
- **Not urgent but important**: While not urgent, these tasks may be valuable to ongoing projects. Block time for them.
- **Urgent but not important**: These tasks can be unpredictable, like a last-minute meeting or a fire you need to put out. Determine if you can delegate them.
- **Not important and not urgent**: Remove these tasks from your to-do list or delegate them.

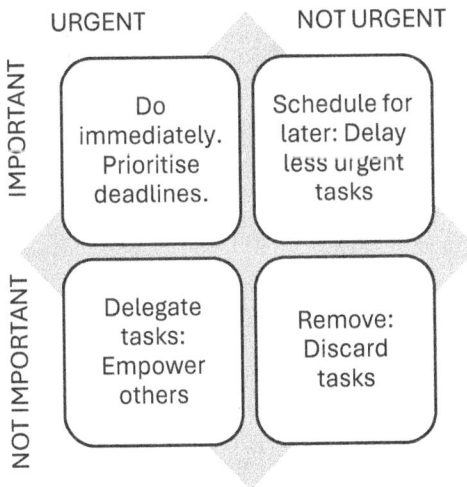

Figure 10: Eisenhower Matrix for time management.

I know that many people struggle with time management, but it is a skill that needs to be nurtured due to its importance for managing people and delivering results.

Identifying High-Impact Tasks

In 1896, an Italian economist named Vilfredo Pareto was studying wealth distribution in Italy. He noticed something striking, roughly 80% of the land was owned by just 20% of the population.

Intrigued, he looked for patterns elsewhere. He found a similar imbalance in other countries and even in other areas of life; a small proportion of causes often produced most effects. Over time, this observation evolved into what we now call the Pareto Principle, or the 80:20 rule.

The principle isn't a strict law, sometimes the ratio is 70:30 or 90:10, but the key point remains: most results come from a small number of causes.

Putting this in practice, you could:

- Solve the 20% of problems that cause 80% of operational issues.
- Spend time on the 20% of tasks that deliver the most value.
- Coach and support the 20% of team members who drive key outcomes.
- Focus on the 20% of relationships that influence 80% of your success.

Saying 'No' Effectively

New managers and team leaders often feel the pressure to say 'yes' to everything, but as the saying goes, *'You can't please all of the people all of the time.'* Learning to say 'no' is essential for avoiding overwhelm and staying focused on what really matters. Saying 'no' isn't negative; it sets boundaries. By responding directly, even when declining, you demonstrate professionalism and respect through honest communication. Politely turning down lower-priority requests frees you to concentrate on the tasks that must be done and make the biggest impact.

> *"I set boundaries to win."*

Meeting or No-Meetings?

'Death by PowerPoint' is bad, but 'death by meetings' is just as painful. Too many gatherings waste time. Before arranging one, ask yourself: *'Is this really necessary?'* Use email or a short video for updates, coffee or lunch for building relationships, and meetings only for brainstorming or gathering key perspectives.

I found that keeping meeting participants small really works; ideally three to seven people, with five being best. This allows everyone to contribute without losing focus, as larger groups make it easy for people to drift off or get distracted.

Set Measurable Objectives

In *2023 State of Goal Setting* report by Microsoft (via Forrester Consulting), 214 enterprise senior executives across retail, healthcare, manufacturing and financial services were surveyed. The findings show that 77 % believe improving the ability to track goal progress and milestones drives better outcomes, and 73 % say increased alignment across the company through better visibility improves their goal-setting and management process.

The following frameworks are some of the most useful to consider when setting measurable objectives. While this book does not delve into detailed explanations, a brief overview of each is provided, along with examples of sectors or cases where they are particularly effective:

- **SMART**: Specific, Measurable, Achievable, Relevant, Time-bound; provides a clear structure for practical and trackable goals, widely applicable across all sectors.

- **OKR**: Objectives and Key Results; sets objectives with measurable key results; useful in tech, start-ups, and innovative organisations to align teams and drive performance.

- **CLEAR**: Collaborative, Limited, Emotional, Appreciable, Refinable; encourages adaptability and motivation, particularly effective in creative or fast-moving environments.

- **FAST**: Frequently discussed, Ambitious, Specific, Transparent; emphasises regular review and transparency, ideal for dynamic teams and project-driven organisations.

- **KPI-driven planning**: Focuses on quantifiable performance indicators linked to strategic outcomes;

commonly used in corporate, retail, and operational management contexts.

- **Outcome-based thinking**: Starts with the desired result and works backwards to define actions; valuable in problem-solving, strategic planning, and project management scenarios.

> **Takeaway**: When objectives are measurable and visibility is high, businesses are more likely to gain alignment and drive performance.

Balancing Short-Term and Long-Term Objectives

Managers must balance short-term needs, like meeting deadlines, with long-term goals, such as growth and sustainability. Allocating time to both ensures immediate productivity while building a foundation for the future.

You might be wondering: How do you balance these? Here's an example from a customer service desk. Suppose you manage a team of 10 and have a metric to answer 80% of calls within 3 minutes, but you're currently achieving 72%. Meanwhile, you know your company is expanding to a new region in 6 months. What do you do?

First, focus on reaching that 80% target. Identify issues, improve processes, and train your team, but don't push for 90%, it's not necessary right now. Then plan, as calls increase with expansion, assess how systems can scale and whether more resources or hires are needed. This takes time, so make your case and get approval for additional budget.

This is how you balance short-term results with long-term planning.

Managing The Shift: Peer to Manager

Transitioning From Peer to Manager

When Satya Nadella became CEO of Microsoft in 2014, he faced the challenge of moving from peer to manager. Before stepping into a leadership role, many of his colleagues had been his equals, and now, as a manager, his responsibilities were radically different. One of his key challenges was clarifying his new role and ensuring both he and his team understood the shift in dynamics.

This transition required:

1) **Shifting relationships**: Nadella could no longer treat colleagues as equals; he was now accountable for their performance.
2) **Balancing authority and trust**: He needed to assert his leadership while maintaining the respect and trust of those he once worked beside.
3) **Mindset change**: Instead of focusing on doing the work himself, Nadella had to focus on enabling his team to succeed.

He credits much of his success to active listening and clear communication, which helped clarify roles and responsibilities for both him and his team.

My experience affirms that the shift from a peer to manager is one of the toughest transitions for any new leader.

Managing Peer Relationships and Establishing Authority

As a newly promoted manager or a team leader, it is essential to clarify your role and set boundaries with former peers. Maintaining trust while asserting *"I lead with respect, not distance."* authority is crucial. Clear and open communication about your expectations will help everyone better understand the new dynamic.

For example, when I was promoted to a leadership role in an international role, the country head asked me to move from an open-plan desk to an office. Initially, I questioned this change, but he explained that in that region, a manager's office sends a signal of authority and leadership. This small shift helped clarify my role in the eyes of my team.

Establishing Boundaries: Friend Versus Boss

As a new leader, it's natural to feel torn between the friendly colleague you once were and the leader you now need to become. You can't maintain the same relationships you had as a peer, so setting clear professional boundaries is essential. For example, if you used to socialise with colleagues outside of work, you might now need to politely step back from certain conversations or decisions to remain impartial. It's about finding a balance, remaining approachable and supportive but also leading with authority and fairness. It's never easy, but over time, your team will respect and understand these boundaries.

Balancing Empathy with Objectivity

While empathy is vital, a leader must also make tough decisions. In my first managers role, I had to make clear decisions regarding a peer who repeatedly failed to meet expectations. Although we had a friendly relationship, I had to clarify my role and ensure accountability. This experience helped establish my authority as a manager who could make tough, fair decisions.

Clarifying Roles and Responsibilities

Understanding Your New Role

As a leader, your work is no longer just about completing tasks. It is about helping your team succeed, because your success now depends on theirs. It is important to be open about this shift and to communicate it clearly, so everyone understands the new focus.

According to Peter F. Drucker, 'Management is doing things right; leadership is doing the right things'. To lead effectively, you need to make roles and responsibilities clear. As Max DePree (former CEO, Herman Miller, USA) said, 'The first responsibility of a leader is to define reality'.

Take the time to ensure every team member knows your role, your goals, and how your work fits into the bigger

> *"When my team wins, I win."*

picture. When your team understands this, it becomes easier to guide and support.

Clarifying Team Roles and Responsibilities

Once you know what your own role is, the next step is making sure everyone on your team knows theirs. This isn't just about job titles; it's about being clear on who does what, who makes decisions, and where responsibilities start and end. Without this clarity, tasks can get duplicated, things can fall through the cracks, and people can feel frustrated or unsure of how to contribute.

For example, imagine a marketing team working on a product launch. If two team members both assume they oversee social media content, you might end up with overlapping posts or conflicting messages. Meanwhile, another task, like coordinating with designers, might get neglected because everyone thought someone else was handling it. By clearly defining roles, such as 'Alice creates the social media plan, Bob approves content, and Carla liaises with the design team', each person knows what they are responsible for and can focus on their area.

Simple tools like Responsible, Accountable, Consulted and Informed (RACI) charts or responsibility matrices can help make this explicit, but even a clear conversation in a team meeting can do wonders. When roles are well defined, team members take ownership of their work, collaboration becomes smoother, and everyone understands how their efforts contribute to the bigger picture.

Figure 11 shows what RACI chart might look like for the marketing team example mentioned above.

Task/Responsibility	Alice	Bob	Carla
Create social media plan	R	C	I
Approve social media content	A	R	I
Liaise with design team	I	C	R
Coordinate overall product launch	C	C	A
Review launch progress	I	I	A

Key:

- R – Responsible: The person who completes the task.
- A – Accountable: The person ultimately answerable for the task's success.
- C – Consulted: People whose input is sought before a decision or action.
- I – Informed: People who need to be kept up to date.

Figure 11: RACI chart for a small marketing team.

Shifting Your Mindset: From Doing Tasks to Leading People

Olivia excelled at school, college, and university, completing all her tasks independently. Homework, assignments, exam revision; she managed it all herself and often found solutions on her own. This reflects the Western education model, which produces strong individual contributors, but this is not enough for most workplaces.

However, as a new team leader in the workplace, Olivia's success depends on collaboration. Teams must communicate and share knowledge to achieve common goals. Leadership adds another layer: you must be people-oriented and collaborative. Olivia needs to adapt from being individual contributor to helping others, in other words. She needs to think of herself as an initiator, enabler, or orchestrator!

Figure 12 shows how you need to shift from being task-oriented to people-oriented.

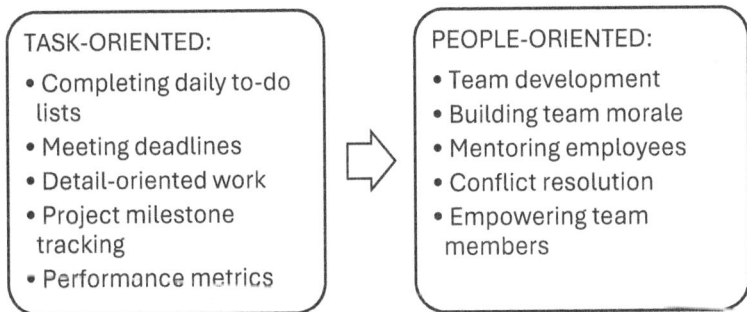

TASK-ORIENTED:
• Completing daily to-do lists
• Meeting deadlines
• Detail-oriented work
• Project milestone tracking
• Performance metrics

PEOPLE-ORIENTED:
• Team development
• Building team morale
• Mentoring employees
• Conflict resolution
• Empowering team members

Figure 12: Shifting from being-task oriented to people-oriented.

Thinking Strategically Versus Operationally

Managers and team leaders must balance the operational demands of daily tasks with a long-term view for the future. Clarifying your team's role within the broader department or unit's strategy ensures that everyone is working towards the same goals, with clear responsibilities aligned to those objectives.

As emphasised earlier in the book, it's not just top executives who are visionary and think strategically. Every level of the company exhibits these qualities, including managers and team leaders like you. For example, a retail manager ensures daily store operations run smoothly (operational) while analysing sales trends to plan which products to stock for seasonal growth and long-term profitability (strategic).

Customer Service: A Leadership Priority

Outstanding customer service isn't just a department; it is the heartbeat of any organisation. Every interaction, from answering an email to resolving a complaint, shapes trust, loyalty, and reputation. For example, a café remembering a regular customer's favourite order or an online retailer resolving a delivery issue quickly can make all the difference.

Core principles include empathy, active listening, clear communication, responsiveness, and taking ownership of outcomes. Leaders set the tone by empowering their teams to act decisively and learn from feedback. Organisations that prioritise service not only delight customers but also build stronger teams, encourage innovation, and secure long-term growth.

Identify and Build on Quick Wins

When Jacinda Ardern became Prime Minister of New Zealand in 2017, she focused on quick, visible wins to build credibility. One of her first actions was passing a law guaranteeing paid parental leave, directly benefiting families. She also responded swiftly and empathetically to crises like the Whakaari/White Island eruption and the Christchurch Mosque attacks, showing clear, compassionate leadership. By combining immediate, high-impact actions with a long-term vision, Ardern earned trust, demonstrated competence, and rallied both her team and the public behind her agenda.

Building early achievements is a powerful way to establish yourself as an effective leader. Focus on small, impactful projects that showcase your leadership skills, engage your team, and celebrate those milestones!

Identifying Quick Wins: Small But Meaningful Contributions

Concentrate on small, high-impact tasks, such as resolving process inefficiencies or clarifying roles. These quick wins demonstrate your capability and commitment to enhancing the team, even when large-scale changes are not immediately feasible.

Organisation-wide research by PwC in 2024 found that employees who set modest short-term goals, for example completing a single slide deck in a day, were more likely to achieve broader performance targets and reported higher levels of job satisfaction.

Prioritising Initiatives with Visible Impact

Select tasks or projects that can produce visible, positive outcomes in the short term. These should align with immediate needs and be achievable quickly.

Early wins are great for shaping how others see you. They show you can make a real impact while also building momentum for the bigger challenges to come.

Recognising Early Efforts of Your Team

Do celebrate your team's efforts as they happen. Spotting and acknowledging small wins in real time, whether in meetings, emails, or one-on-one chats, boosts morale and shows that you notice their dedication. Early recognition helps your team stay motivated and demonstrates that you are a supportive leader who values ongoing contributions.

Reporting Early Successes

Perception shapes decisions; that's the cold and brutal reality in business. As a new leader, it's not just your team you need to manage, but how others see you as well. I've learnt that you must blow your own trumpet, as no one else will, so, make it a habit to share those wins with senior leadership.

Regular updates that tie your progress to department or unit goals build your credibility and show you're delivering on your promises. These updates let people see the real impact of your work.

Consider this example, one new manager I worked with started sending brief weekly summaries highlighting completed projects and measurable results; within a few months, senior leaders were referencing his achievements in wider team meetings, which boosted his visibility and influence. I thought this was a great idea!

Celebrating Achievements

Take the time to recognise achievements in a way that suits everyone. Some team members enjoy public praise, while others respond better to a private word of thanks. Focus on the behaviours that made the success possible, such as creativity, collaboration, or initiative. Remember, it's free to say, *'Thank you'*.

Be mindful of how and where you celebrate successes. While after-work drinks are common in some Western workplaces, not everyone participates for personal or religious reasons. If a team member does not drink, it's important to choose inclusive ways to celebrate rather than automatically arranging a night out in a bar. Simple, thoughtful recognition during work hours can be just as meaningful.

Chapter 6: Driving Team Performance and Continuous Growth

Address Morale or Performance Issues

Sir Mark Grundy (Principal, Shireland Collegiate Academy and George Salter, UK) faced a dramatic leadership challenge when his schools fell from outstanding to being placed in Ofsted's special measures. Grundy admitted he had taken his *'eye off the ball'*. He rallied staff, reset expectations, and rebuilt systems, culture and accountability. Within a year, the schools regained top ratings.

This story shows that setbacks, even after success, can become growth opportunities. Calm leadership, clear vision, collaboration and openness to change allow managers to turn challenges into progress. Prioritising resilience and clear communication strengthen both leaders and their teams, preparing them to face future obstacles with confidence.

Understanding Human Behaviour

Understanding what makes humans tick will help you manage them better. Human behaviour cannot be modelled like machines, as people have thoughts, feelings, and emotions that cannot be quantified.

Al-Ghazali (philosopher and theologian, modern-day Iran, d. 1111 CE) presents a fascinating model of human needs, as shown in Figure 13. He argues that basic needs must be met first before anything else.

Figure 13: Al-Ghazali's model of human needs.

Ibn Khaldun (historian and philosopher, modern-day Tunisia, d. 1406 CE) expanded on this idea by outlining a hierarchy of needs, beginning with necessities, followed by comfort, and finally luxuries. Giambattista Vico (philosopher, Italy, d. 1744) developed the concept further, and later, Maslow (psychologist, USA, d. 1970) refined it into his well-known hierarchy of needs, as shown in Figure 14.

In times of uncertainty, your team may feel anxious or worried about their future, as it challenges their sense of security. For example, if the company's financial situation is unstable and executives are considering organisational changes, the possibility of job losses can be deeply unsettling. This concern naturally affects how people behave at work; their focus, motivation, and creativity can all be impacted. This emotional response aligns with the hierarchy of needs, which thinkers like Al-Ghazali, Ibn Khaldun, Giambattista Vico, and Maslow emphasised: basic needs must be met before higher-level goals can be pursued. When people feel their survival is at risk, it's harder for them to perform at their best.

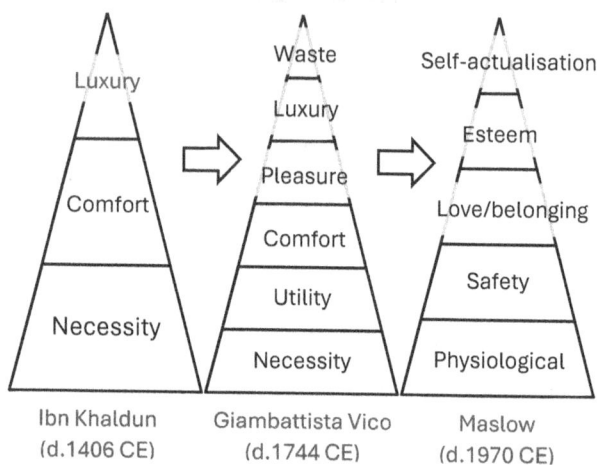

Figure 14: Ibn Khaldun's and Maslow's hierarchy of needs models.

As a leader, sensitivity and empathy are vital. Acknowledging your team's concerns and offering reassurance creates a safe, supportive environment. In my experience, leaders who understand their team's emotions consistently achieve better results.

Emotional Challenges for New Leaders

Transitioning into leadership can trigger self-doubt, frustration, or moments of panic, and handling these emotions is vital for personal performance and team morale. As Pema Chödrön (Buddhist teacher and author, USA) notes, *'The most fundamental aggression to ourselves ... is to remain ignorant by not having the courage to look at ourselves honestly and gently'.* Meeting emotions directly and reflecting on one's leadership journey helps to build resilience.

Some discomfort also signals growth. Kathleen Spike (leadership coach and author, USA) remarks, *'There are certain emotions that will kill your drive; frustration means you are on the verge of a breakthrough'.* Feeling stretched or unsettled often indicates progress rather than failure.

Seeking support, using stress-management techniques, and making space for reflection enable leaders to work with their emotions rather than suppress them, laying the groundwork for stronger leadership and a more motivated team.

Top 5 Problem-Solving Frameworks

Solving problems is a core function of all leaders, from team leaders all the way to the highest ranks of organisations. Most problems you should be able to be resolve without tools, but for more complex issues, there are frameworks that may help. For new managers and team leaders, the most *"I respond, not react."* practical problem-solving frameworks are those that are easy to learn, actionable, and focused on people and processes rather than highly technical analysis. Table 6 shows a few problem-solving frameworks that are easy to use.

Other useful frameworks for leaders are in Appendix A.

Table 6: Problem-solving frameworks.

Framework	Details
PDCA (Plan–Do–Check–Act)	**Why:** Encourages a structured, iterative approach to solving problems without being overwhelming. **Use Case:** Process improvements, team workflow adjustments, trial-and-error solutions.
5 Whys	**Why:** Simple and quick method to get to the root cause of problems. **Use Case:** Performance issues, missed deadlines, miscommunications.
Fishbone (Ishikawa) Diagram	**Why:** Visual and collaborative; helps identify multiple causes of a problem. **Use Case:** Team productivity challenges, recurring mistakes, or quality issues.
Design Thinking (Simplified Version)	**Why:** Encourages empathy and understanding of team or customer needs before acting. **Use Case:** Improving team engagement, designing workflows, or creating small process innovations.
DMAIC (Define–Measure–Analyse–Improve–Control) – Simplified	**Why:** Provides a structured, step-by-step problem-solving approach using data and observation. **Use Case:** Tracking performance metrics, improving efficiency, or standardising team processes.

Avoid complex frameworks like TRIZ or overly strategic consulting models (like full McKinsey 7-step) initially, they are too abstract for day-to-day team management. Focus on frameworks that allow quick wins, visualisation, and team participation.

Turning Mistakes into Teaching Moments

Thomas Edison (inventor and businessman, USA) famously remarked about his attempts to invent the light bulb, *'I have not failed. I've just found 10,000 ways that won't work'*.

Setbacks provide valuable insights. Reflect on errors, extract lessons, and encourage your team to do the same. By viewing challenges as opportunities for growth, you develop resilience and promote a culture of continuous improvement.

Common Pitfalls for New Managers

I've made many mistakes and learnt from them. It is expected that you too will make mistakes in your new role, after all, we are humans! However, the goal is to reduce these. A few areas where you should not repeat my mistakes are related to micromanaging, not delegating, avoiding tough conversations and taking credit that others deserve. Here are some tips to deal with these issues:

- **Micromanagement**: Focus on the result; let your team or individuals figure out the best way to get the job done. You will be surprised how people can deliver if they are left to their own devices. Bill Gates (co-founder of Microsoft and philanthropist, USA) once famously said, *'I choose a lazy person to do a hard job. Because a lazy person will find an easy way to do it'*.

- **Delegating:** Remind yourself each morning that you're now a leader and your team can deliver. There's no need to get your 'hands dirty' (meant in a nice way) unless necessary!

- **Tough conversations:** Tough discussions aren't always about saying 'no' or being harsh. Sometimes, they're about asking the right questions:

  'Are you sure about this?'

  'What happens if it doesn't work out?'

  'Is there an alternative option or route?'

  'Who will be responsible for this?'

  Asking these questions encourages accountability and helps people think critically.

- **Taking credit:** Another common mistake is taking credit for successes instead of recognising the efforts of your team. Good leaders will always attribute success to their team's collective efforts, and it won't go amiss as your line manager and above see your teams success as your success!

Introduce Consistent Communication Practices

Effective communication is the foundation of strong leadership. It involves not only speaking clearly but also listening actively, engaging empathetically, and ensuring your team feels informed and supported. Rehmah Kasule (founder,

CEDA International, Uganda) embodies this approach. Leading a non-profit that empowers youth and women across East Africa, she says, *'As a leader, if you do not listen to what people are saying, you are leading blindly'*. So, its by engaging with communities, asking tough questions, and using storytelling to make messages resonate, that she builds trust and creates a shared vision.

Communication is central to managerial success. Clear, influential, and trustworthy messaging, coupled with active listening and collaboration, drives results. Managers must handle difficult conversations and provide constructive feedback. They must communicate effectively, including in remote or hybrid settings. As Richard Branson (entrepreneur and founder of Virgin Group, UK) observes, *'Communication is the most important skill any leader can possess'*.

Structuring Messages for Clarity

Juliet Bouverie (Chief Executive, Stroke Association, UK) demonstrates the importance of structured, transparent communication. She held open 'Ask Juliet' sessions, shadowed frontline colleagues, and used video blogs to share key messages and reflections.

Clear communication begins with organising your thoughts and focusing on key points. Avoid unnecessary details, as this ensures the team understands the message and knows how to act on it.

Keep your message simple and direct, so there's no room for confusion or misinterpretation.

Using Concise, Professional Language

Leaders should always aim to use straightforward, professional language. Avoid jargon or ambiguous terms that might confuse listeners. The marketing world offers strong examples: Nike's 'Just Do It' and BMW's 'The Ultimate Driving Machine' show the power of concise, clear messaging. In international teams, be mindful of language choices, avoiding colloquialisms and complex phrasing. For instance, say *'Are you saying...?'* rather than *'Are you insinuating...?'*

> *"I say more with less."*

Persuasive Techniques for New Leaders

As a new leader, you may not have the authority to dictate every decision, but you can still influence others effectively. Peter Linden (Director, Global Learning Solutions Director, Hult Ashridge, UK) is a strong advocator of this concept. He says, *'In times of change, leaders who listen deeply, connect widely, and act with purpose and consistency can influence far beyond hierarchical authority.'*

Hult Ashridge provides key steps for influencing without authority:

- **Understand the landscape**: Identify key stakeholders, formal and informal power dynamics, and areas of potential resistance.
- **Connect to their needs**: Frame proposals in terms of stakeholders' specific interests and priorities.

- **Be a value creator:** Offer proactive solutions that address organisational and individual pain points.
- **Find advocates:** Build trust and rapport with allies who can champion the change.
- **Be a reliable partner:** Demonstrate integrity, competence, and follow-through to earn support.

Effective Email and Virtual Team Practices

In remote teams, communication must be even clearer. Use direct, inclusive language in emails, ensure everyone is included in key communications, and maintain open dialogue. Video calls enhance engagement and presence, allowing teams to connect as if in person. Encourage cameras on to replicate in-person dynamics and encourage accountability.

Establish Feedback Mechanisms

Regular feedback is essential for improving performance, spotting problems early, and keeping teams aligned. It doesn't have to be formal; frequent, two-way feedback often works best.

For example, a project manager might hold a daily 15-minute stand-up to share updates and obstacles, while a marketing lead might request peer feedback on a campaign draft before it goes live. A variety of tools can support this process:

- Communication platforms like Slack, Microsoft Teams, or Workplace allow quick, informal feedback and discussion threads.

- Visual collaboration tools such as Miro or Trello enable teams to comment on tasks, highlight blockers, and track progress.

- Survey and polling tools like Google Forms, Typeform, or Mentimeter provide anonymous ways for team members to give honest feedback.

- Performance management software such as Lattice, 15Five, or Culture Amp helps formalise 1:1s, 360° feedback, and goal tracking.

Let's briefly see how great leaders use feedback. Murat Ülker (CEO, Yıldız Holding, Türkiye) uses structured systems, including a 360° process, to encourage open dialogue across all levels, creating a safe space for employees to share views. Johnny Warström (CEO, Mentimeter, Sweden) built a feedback-rich culture from the start, combining formal and informal loops to understand what works, what needs improving, and how staff feel about their work.

Timing and Tone Best Practices

The *HBR Guide to Coaching Employees* published in 2014 notes that public criticism can trigger a 'threat response' in employees. When people feel threatened, they focus on defending themselves rather than learning from feedback, which reduces effectiveness and can harm engagement.

The timing and tone of feedback are important. Give feedback promptly while the event is still fresh. Choose an appropriate setting for sensitive feedback; private conversations are usually more effective than public ones, as no one wants to be embarrassed in front of colleagues. Keep your tone supportive and non-judgmental to maintain trust and respect.

Table 7 shows how you can better phrase your feedback to your team member.

Table 7: Effective phrases for feedback.

Unhelpful Phrasing	Effective Phrasing
You're doing this wrong.	I noticed this could be improved; here's one way to approach it.
That's not good enough.	Let's review this section together and see how it can be strengthened.
Why didn't you do it properly?	I see what you attempted; here's an adjustment that could work better.
You need to fix this.	Consider revising this part to align with the goal; here's an example.
You always make mistakes here.	I've noticed this part is tricky; let's work on it together.
This is a disaster.	Here's how we can improve it.
You clearly don't understand.	Let's go over this concept again to make sure it's clear.
Stop doing it like that.	Try this alternative approach.
You're slow at this.	Let's look at streamlining for efficiency.
This isn't acceptable.	We need to adjust to meet the standard.

Implement and Monitor Plans

Breaking Down Objectives

Translate high-level goals into actionable steps, assign ownership, and set measurable milestones. Use tools like

Trello, Asana, or responsibility matrices to track progress. Regular check-ins, whether daily stand-ups or weekly reviews, keep the team on course and highlight challenges early.

Monitoring Progress and Adjusting Course

Monitoring involves tracking performance metrics and adjusting where necessary. For example, a sales manager launching a new campaign might track lead conversion rates weekly, while a product manager could compare development milestones against the roadmap. Table 8 shows an example of performance metrics tracking.

These measures allow leaders to spot deviations early, make corrections, and maintain momentum toward goals.

Annika Falkengren (former CEO of SEB, Sweden) emphasised close monitoring of strategic initiatives. She implemented detailed performance dashboards and weekly leadership review meetings to track progress across business units. By acting quickly when deviations occurred, she ensured initiatives remained aligned with long-term goals while maintaining operational efficiency.

Similarly, Lei Jun (founder of Xiaomi, China), is known for rigorous execution practices. During new product launches, Xiaomi teams use sprint-based planning and daily check-ins to monitor progress. If an issue arises, immediate adjustments are made, whether reallocating development resources or redesigning marketing campaigns. This approach allows the company to bring innovative products to market rapidly while maintaining high standards.

Table 8: Performance metrics tracking.

Step	Action / Who	Metrics - Indicators / Review Frequency
1. Break down goals	Convert objectives into actionable tasks /**Manager**	Number of tasks defined; clarity of responsibilities /**Planning session**
2. Assign ownership	Allocate tasks to specific team members /**Manager**	Tasks assigned with deadlines /**At assignment**
3. Set milestones	Define measurable checkpoints /**Manager** and **Team**	Milestones defined and aligned to objectives /**Kick-off meeting**
4. Track progress	Use tools like Trello, Asana /**Team**	Completion %, blockers, delays /**Daily / Weekly**
5. Regular check-ins	Stand-ups or weekly reviews to update progress /**Manager** and **Team**	Attendance, blockers addressed, decisions made /**Daily / Weekly**
6. Adjust plans	Reallocate resources or modify tasks /**Manager**	Corrective actions executed /**As needed**
7. Share progress	Communicate status openly with the team /**Manager**	Team awareness, engagement levels /**Weekly updates**
8. Celebrate success	Recognise achievements and contributions /**Manager**	Morale indicators, recognition delivered /**Milestone or project completion**
9. Gather feedback	Collect lessons learned for continuous improvement /**Manager** and **Team**	Feedback quality, actionable insights / **End-of-project**

Transparency and Team Engagement

Sharing progress with your team, celebrating successes, and discussing obstacles openly strengthens trust and engagement. When employees see that plans are actively monitored, adjustments are made thoughtfully, and achievements are recognised, it reinforces accountability and builds confidence in your leadership.

Reinforce Good Leadership and Accountability

Making Timely, Accountable Decisions

In fast-paced environments, decisions must be both quick and well-informed. Gather relevant data, consult your team when necessary, and act decisively. Quick decisions are essential in some situations, but accuracy ensures that choices stand up to scrutiny. Assessing risks and rewards before deciding helps you anticipate potential pitfalls and prepare for challenges.

Knowing when to involve others is equally important:

- **High-impact decisions**: Seek input from your team or stakeholders.
- **Time-sensitive or clear-cut issues**: Decide on your own.

Balancing consultation with independent action demonstrates accountability and strengthens confidence in your leadership.

Encouraging Team Ownership and Innovation

Involving your team in decision-making promotes engagement, accountability, and creativity. Ask for input and encourage new ideas. Research by the Institute of Labour Economics in Bonn, Germany, found that employees who feel ownership show lower turnover, stronger identification with company goals, and a greater willingness to act in the organisation's best interests. Encouraging ownership empowers teams and creates a culture of shared responsibility.

Exercise Decisive Leadership

Being able to make firm, confident decisions is a hallmark of effective leadership. Leaders who hesitate risk stagnation, while decisive leaders inspire confidence, motivate their teams, and drive results. Research among 350 global companies shows that top performers excel not only in strategic decisions, such as market entry, acquisitions, or resource allocation, but also in critical operational choices that shape day-to-day success, from innovating products to managing partners efficiently.

Accepting Responsibility

Mistakes are inevitable, but leaders must take responsibility for their actions and decisions. Acknowledge errors and avoid blaming others. Importantly, you must proactively correct issues. Demonstrating accountability sets a strong example for your team.

In one of my roles, I was selling complex software alongside a global vendor to one of the largest oil and gas companies in the world. Although the software had been sold successfully, we encountered significant implementation issues. Client threatened to blacklist us for 10 years if we did not fix the issues. Upon hearing this, my vendor counterpart suggested, *'This is going to end very badly for both of us, let's blame our sales team members'*. I responded firmly that I refused to blame anyone wrongly and it was something that I would take full responsibility for! The issues were eventually resolved amicably, and trust with my team was strengthened.

Sharing Lessons to Improve Team Performance

Creating a culture where teams can openly discuss mistakes is crucial for growth. Research at Cambridge Judge Business School found that teams reflecting on errors and sharing insights improved both creative problem-solving and overall performance. Leaders can encourage this by emphasising on transparency, seeing mistakes as learning opportunities, and encouraging team-wide reflection.

Defending Your Team

Leaders must protect their team members strongly when they are unfairly blamed or criticised. In one situation, a senior manager reprimanded my team member for an issue my team member did not cause. I intervened

> "I face the storm so they can work in calm."

immediately and said publicly, *'Even if a mistake had been made, I cannot allow my team to be treated like this. I will take full responsibility'*. This action protected my team member, who genuinely thanked me privately for having his back. Since that day, my reputation as a fierce defender of the team grew, and it really motivated everyone – and me!

Offer Coaching and Recognition

Good leaders understand that coaching and recognition are central to building engagement and improving performance, as well as developing talent. Coaching involves guiding team members to improve skills and overcome obstacles while recognition reinforces desired behaviours and motivates individuals to excel.

Practical Coaching in Action

Coaching does not always mean formal training sessions. It often involves regular one-on-one conversations, providing constructive feedback, and helping employees reflect on challenges and solutions. For instance, Caroline Cirillo (CEO, Kuehne+Nagel, Switzerland) regularly holds structured mentoring sessions with senior managers to guide strategic decision-making and leadership development, encouraging reflective learning across the organisation.

Recognition That Drives Engagement

Recognising achievements, both big and small, strengthens morale and reinforces high performance. Global examples of coaching and recognition come from Emma Walmsley (CEO, GSK, UK), who emphasises regular feedback loops, pairing coaching sessions with recognition of innovative research and leadership contributions, creating a culture of learning and achievement.

Ola Källenius (CEO and Chairman, Mercedes-Benz Group, Germany) encourages managers to coach teams on innovation and sustainability initiatives while celebrating milestones publicly, ensuring both skill development and recognition are part of everyday leadership practice.

> **Lesson:** Even small, sincere acknowledgments can significantly improve motivation, energy, engagement, and retention.

Build Cross-Departmental Relationships

Gillian Tans (CEO, Booking.com, Netherlands) is a great believer in collaboration. She encouraged product, marketing, and data teams to collaborate closely, thereby embedding cross-departmental communication into the company's culture. This ensured seamless customer experiences and faster execution of strategic initiatives.

The lesson is very clear here; strong leaders know that success rarely comes from working in isolation. Building relationships across departments is crucial for promoting collaboration, improving efficiency, and driving organisational goals.

What Cross-Department Collaboration Provides

Collaboration across departments allows teams to leverage diverse expertise, anticipate challenges, and identify opportunities that might otherwise be missed. For example, when a marketing team partners closely with product development, campaigns can be tailored to highlight the product's most compelling features, while customer feedback flows seamlessly to improve future iterations.

Practical Steps to Build Relationships

- **Engage proactively**: Take the initiative to meet colleagues in other functions. Regular check-ins, joint workshops, or even informal coffee chats can establish trust and open channels for communication.

- **Understand other teams' priorities**: Knowing what drives other departments help you anticipate their needs and align your goals, thus avoiding conflicts.

- **Share knowledge and resources**: Providing expertise, insights, or tools to another team builds goodwill and encourages reciprocal support.

- **Facilitate joint problem-solving**: Involving multiple departments in decision-making or problem-solving sessions ensures better solutions.

Tip: I found that developing personal relationships with counterparts in other departments makes difficult situations easier to handle and allows more open, transparent communication.

THE ESSENTIAL GUIDE FOR NEW MANAGERS AND TEAM LEADERS

Identify and Address Skill Gaps

James Mwangi (CEO, Equity Bank, Kenya) has emphasised developing team capabilities by rotating managers across departments and pairing junior staff with senior mentors. This hands-on coaching helps identify skill gaps early while building leadership capacity across the organisation.

In similar manner, José Antonio Fernández (CEO, Grupo Modelo, Mexico) implemented targeted training programs for emerging leaders while recognising team achievements publicly. This approach both addresses skill gaps and strengthens motivation and engagement.

As a new team leader or a manger, you will need to assess skill gaps at some point as you settle in, understand team strengths, and plan to expand or scale effectively. Get used to this idea.

Matching Tasks to Team Capabilities

Delegation is a critical skill for new managers. I recommend creating a quick visual heatmap of your team's skills. This will help you match tasks to their abilities. Table 9 shows what such a heatmap might look like.

The example in the table is for managing a team building AI agents for healthcare. Start by creating a skills heatmap (or matrix if you prefer non-visuals) to guide task assignments. Use simple tools like spreadsheets to do this quickly. Be sure to speak with each team member to understand their skills and cross-check with others for accuracy.

Table 9: Skills heatmap.

Skill	David	Ahmad	Jenny	Wei	Gita
Healthcare Domain Knowledge					
Machine Learning & Deep Learning					
Natural Language Processing (NLP)					
Medical Data Analysis and Processing					
Clinical Decision Support Systems (CDSS)					
Data Privacy and Security (HIPAA, GDPR)					
Computer Vision (for medical imaging)					
AI Ethics and Bias Mitigation					
Reinforcement Learning (for tailored treatment)					
Interdisciplinary Collaboration					

Key Strong   Weak

Empower Your Team by Trusting Them

Trust is central to effective delegation. When team members feel trusted, they are more likely to take initiative, deliver quality work, and go the extra mile. For instance, as a sales unit head, I was given significant autonomy by a respected executive. His trust empowered me to make key decisions, which boosted my morale, job satisfaction, accountability, and creativity. I applied the same principle with my own teams, often resulting in annual sales targets being exceeded by substantial margins.

Conduct A 30-Day or 60-Day Review

A review is an important checkpoint for new managers and team leaders. It allows you to take stock of what has been achieved, identify areas for improvement, and adjust plans for the next phase. The review should consider team performance, progress against objectives, and personal development as a leader. For example, after completing a quarterly project, a manager might review how well deadlines were met, which team members exceeded expectations, and whether any processes could be streamlined, using these insights to plan more effectively for the next quarter.

Team and Individual Feedback

Use the review to solicit feedback from team members. Encouraging honest input about processes, leadership style, and challenges is crucial. For example, a frontline retail team member might share that stock replenishment takes longer than expected or that clearer instructions would help during peak hours. Patrick Pouyanné (CEO, TotalEnergies, France) implements quarterly reflection sessions with managers across business units to assess both project outcomes and leadership effectiveness. This approach not only identifies gaps but also reinforces a culture of continuous improvement.

Personal Leadership Evaluation

The 30-day or 60-day review should also include self-assessment. Reflect on what went well, what could have been done differently, and how your management style impacts your team. Consider feedback from mentors or peers to gain perspective. Strive Masiyiwa (founder, Econet Group, Zimbabwe) attributes part of his leadership success to regularly reviewing decisions, team dynamics, and personal development to ensure he stays effective in guiding a growing organisation.

> **Takeaway:** A 30-day or 60-Day review is more than a formality. Done well, it strengthens team alignment, uncovers skill gaps, and allows you to recalibrate your approach for the next period and beyond.

Communicate a Forward-Looking Roadmap

Once the initial period is complete and your team is aligned, it's essential to clearly communicate a forward-looking roadmap. This helps set expectations and provide direction, as well as motivating your team around shared objectives. For example, an engineering team leader might outline upcoming project milestones, such as completing design phases and meeting safety standards showing each team member how their work contributes to the successful delivery of the project.

Define Clear Priorities

A roadmap should highlight key objectives, milestones, and the rationale behind them. It creates a sense of purpose and ensures everyone understands how their work contributes to organisational goals. Emma Walmsley has a habit of regularly communicating multi-year plans to her teams, breaking down large initiatives into clear steps while showing how they align with long-term corporate strategy.

Engage the Team in Planning

Inviting input from team members when shaping the roadmap helps to develop creative solutions and allows anticipation of potential challenges. Luis Alberto Moreno (former President, Inter-American Development Bank, Colombia) credits part of his success to involving senior staff in strategic planning discussions, ensuring initiatives were realistic and supported across departments.

Use Multiple Channels and Clarity of Messaging

Communicating a roadmap effectively requires clear, consistent messaging. You should utilise visual aids, presentations, and collaborative platforms to help reinforce priorities. Patrick Collison (Co-founder, Stripe, Ireland/USA) ensures that strategic goals and product roadmaps are shared transparently with teams using both written updates and interactive discussions, enabling alignment and accountability.

Best Practices for Hiring and Firing!

No guide on managing people would be complete without addressing best practices for hiring new team members and managing exits with dignity. As a manager, whether new or experienced, these responsibilities will form part of your role, even if you don't need to recruit or let people go straight away.

This section won't cover detailed HR or recruitment procedures, as those vary by organisation and are best handled through your internal HR department. Instead, what you'll find here are practical pieces of advice to help you approach hiring and employee exits with fairness, clarity, and professionalism.

Why Do You Need to Hire People?

Hiring happens for a variety of reasons, including:

- **Growth:** Your team may need to expand to handle increased business, higher service demand, or new opportunities.
- **Internal reorganisations:** During structural changes, people move between teams or departments. You may lose team members and need to replace them.
- **Natural turnover:** People leave organisations for many reasons: career progression, retirement, relocation, changes in personal circumstances, or, in some cases, dismissal.

Best Practice for Hiring

When it comes to hiring, here are few practical tips:

- **Don't let others choose for you:** There can be pressure from senior managers to hire certain individuals or to meet preferences. I was once encouraged to hire more women into my sales team, but I couldn't find the right candidate at that time. I hire on merit, not on gender. As the manager, you're responsible for the team's performance, so you must be confident in your choice.

- **Don't hire people simply because they're nice:** Being pleasant is great but it's not enough. Hiring someone who can't deliver will eventually cause problems for you and the team. Make sure they genuinely meet the key requirements of the role, especially in terms of experience and capability.

- **Shared interests are not a hiring criterion:** It can be tempting to choose someone because they support your favourite team or share your hobbies. While it's a nice bonus, it should only be considered after the essential requirements have been met.

- **A face-to-face conversation is invaluable:** Your organisation may use aptitude tests, assessments, or technical evaluations, and these can be useful, especially for highly technical roles. But I always find a face-to-face meeting provides the most insight. An hour over coffee often tells you more about a candidate than any video call or automated test.

Ask simple, practical questions and let the candidate explain their thinking. For example, if I'm hiring an experienced customer service representative, I might ask: *'Have you ever dealt with an angry customer? How did you handle the situation?'* The answer will give you strong clues about whether they're the right fit for the role!

Why Do You Need to Fire People?

At some point in your journey as a leader, you will need to remove people from their roles, either move them to another position within the organisation, or to fire them, in other words, remove them from the organisation. This sounds terrifying for some, but sadly, this is part of leading people, and you better get used to this.

Dismissing someone is always a serious step and should only happen after fair processes, clear communication, and genuine attempts to help the person succeed. But there are legitimate reasons an organisation may need to let someone go.

Poor performance

A major reason, but always a last resort. Before considering dismissal, managers should provide:

- Clear expectations and objectives
- Coaching and feedback
- Training or reskilling
- Opportunities to improve
- Reasonable time for progress

If, after all this, the individual still cannot meet the required standard, keeping them in the role can harm the performance and wellbeing of the wider team.

Lack of compliance or misconduct

If someone consistently fails to meet essential requirements of their role, for example:

- Mishandling sensitive data
- Breaching company policies
- Working with a competitor
- Violating contractual obligations
- Breaking the law

They may face dismissal if issues are not corrected or involve serious misconduct.

Gross misconduct

Severe behaviour that may justify immediate dismissal, such as:

- Theft or fraud
- Violence or threats
- Serious harassment
- Severe breaches of safety
- Intentional data breaches

Redundancy

When the job itself no longer exists due to business changes, restructuring, or financial pressures, not because of the individual's behaviour or ability.

Capability issues (not conduct-related)

Where the person is unable to perform their job due to skill, health, or capacity reasons after all reasonable adjustments and support have been explored.

Statutory or legal restrictions

For example, if someone loses a licence required for their role (e.g., a driver, a financial adviser, a pilot).

Best Practice to Fire People

Dismissing someone is one of the hardest responsibilities any leader faces. It should always be handled with fairness and respect.

Use data to inform your decision

Emotions are part of being human and no one enjoys giving or receiving bad news. Using clear, objective data helps reduce the emotional weight and provides transparency behind the decision.

My approach is always to speak to the person openly, explain the rationale, and walk them through the facts, whether they agree or not. For example, I once had to dismiss a friend because he consistently arrived at 10am instead of the required 9am. The attendance records were clear, and because the data was in front of him, there was no argument. It made the conversation easier for both of us, even though the decision was difficult!

Always treat people with respect

You can treat someone with contempt, or you can treat them with dignity. The difference matters, not just for the individual, but for the reputation of the organisation.

I once witnessed a very poor example at the UK office of a major Japanese company. A woman was called to reception to meet someone, only to find the HR manager waiting to dismiss her on the spot. She wasn't allowed to return to her desk to collect her belongings. She broke down in tears in full view of an open-plan office. It was an HR disaster and deeply damaging to morale.

By contrast, a friend of mine was made redundant from Oracle in the UK in a much more respectful manner. His manager explained the business rationale, gave him three months to find a new role externally, and allowed him to use the office for job searching. It was handled with compassion and professionalism, and it reflected well on Oracle as an employer.

Create a Development Plan for Yourself

Stepping into a leadership role isn't just about managing others; it's about deliberately investing in your own growth. A well-structured personal development plan helps you pinpoint the skills you need to build, track your progress, and set yourself up for long-term success. Unless you happen to inherit a family business empire, no one rises through the ranks by chance or friendship alone, ultimately, advancing as a leader comes down to developing your competence, honing your skills, and sharpening your strategic thinking.

Assess Your Strengths and Development Needs

Jeff Poeppelman (Chief Pilot, Nationwide Aviation Business Center, USA) illustrates the power of proactive self-assessment. He looked beyond his technical expertise, evaluating leadership, communication, delegation, and problem-solving skills in preparation for senior roles. He set clear goals, such as earning the NBAA Certified Aviation Manager (CAM) credential, seeking mentoring, and building complementary soft skills. Going on a development journey prepared him for leadership rather than remaining solely a senior pilot.

"I grow myself to grow my team."

Identifying key skills to grow:

- **Leadership, communication, and delegation**: Focus on inspiring and empowering your team and being clear.
- **Prioritisation**: Concentrate on skills that impact both current performance and future goals. For example, if team collaboration is a challenge, prioritise soft skills in the areas of interpersonal and conflict-resolution.

Seek Feedback and Mentorship

Feedback is essential for growth. You should actively solicit constructive input from colleagues, managers, and team members about your leadership style and effectiveness.

How to make it work:

- **Use one-to-one conversations for sensitive topics**: People are often more candid when not speaking in a group.

- **Frame questions specifically**: *'How could I improve my delegation approach?'* or *'What can I do differently to support the team better?'*

- **Respond positively to feedback**: Avoid defensiveness and think about the steps you may need to take. Showing simple gratitude, such as *'Thank you for your insight,'* encourages open dialogue and strengthens relationships.

Finding mentors and role models is also a valuable for developing your leadership career. Mentors provide guidance, diverse perspectives, and lessons from experience. Start with internal mentorship programmes, if available, or approach your line manager or HR for support.

If none exist, external platforms such as LinkedIn and MentorCruise are valuable alternatives, as shown in Figure 15.

LinkedIn: Use LinkedIn to connect with seasoned professionals in leadership. Reach out to those with experience in the areas you want to develop, such as team management, strategic planning, or change management.

MentorCruise: An online platform where you can connect with mentors who specialise in leadership, management, and other professional skills, offering guidance, feedback, and personalised career development support.

Figure 15: Finding mentors outside your organisation.

Observing experienced leaders is another effective approach. Learning how they handle difficult conversations and strategic decisions can shape your own leadership style. For instance, Strive Masiyiwa, founder of Econet Group in Kenya, emphasises learning by observing others while reflecting critically on each situation to refine his own decision-making.

Set Short- and Long-Term Goals

Practical steps for growth:

- **Short-term goals**: Focus on skills like effective delegation or communication.
- **Long-term goals**: Prepare for higher leadership responsibilities, such as managing multiple teams or strategic projects.

Tracking progress:

- Review goals regularly and celebrate small achievements.
- Adjust plans based on feedback, any emerging challenges, and new opportunities that arise.

Here is a simple example of tracking your progress for the goal of improving delegation:

- **Goal**: Delegate 50% of non-critical tasks in month one, increasing to 70% by month three.
- **Feedback**: Ask team members about clarity and comfort with assigned tasks.
- **Personal reflection**: Track how often you intervene unnecessarily and adjust according to team readiness.

Continuous Learning Approaches

Invest in yourself; attend leadership courses, read books that challenge your thinking, and engage in workshops that sharpen your skills.

Great leaders never stop learning. As John F. Kennedy said, *'Leadership and learning are indispensable to each other'*. Staying ahead requires discipline and the courage to explore new ideas.

"I measure progress, not perfection." The entrepreneur Tim Ferriss talks a lot about how successful people use books to shorten their learning curves. In his book, *Tools of Titans* he shares habits from top performers, many of whom list reading as a major influence on their success.

A Harvard Business Review study shows that leaders who read regularly are better at tackling strategic challenges and making informed decisions. Warren Buffett reportedly spends around 80% of his day reading.

Continuous learning isn't just about picking up technical skills or earning certifications for your current role. It's about keeping an eye on the bigger picture which involves following industry trends, economic forecasts, and even political shifts.

COURSES

- **Harvard Business School Online** – Known for offering high-quality leadership courses such as 'Leadership Principles' and 'Management Essentials.'
- **Coursera** – Offers a wide range of leadership courses from top universities, such as 'Leading People and Teams' by the University of Michigan and 'Foundations of Everyday Leadership' by the University of Illinois.
- **LinkedIn Learning** – Offers practical leadership courses like 'Leading with Emotional Intelligence' and 'Developing Executive Presence.'
- **MIT Sloan Executive Education** – Offers world-class leadership development programs, including 'Advanced Management Program' and 'Transformational Leadership.'

BOOKS

- **'Radical Candor: Be a Kick-Ass Boss Without Losing Your Humanity'** by Kim Scott – Focuses on the importance of open, honest communication in leadership, helping leaders build strong relationships with their teams through caring but direct feedback.
- **'The Five Dysfunctions of a Team'** by Patrick Lencioni – A classic in team building and leadership, explaining the challenges and strategies for leading teams effectively.
- **'Dare to Lead'** by Brené Brown – Focuses on vulnerability, courage, and trust as foundational leadership qualities.
- **'Drive: The Surprising Truth About What Motivates Us'** by Daniel H. Pink – Explores motivation and how it plays a crucial role in leadership and organisational performance.

WORKSHOPS AND SEMINARS

- **Tony Robbins' Leadership Seminars** – Well-known for powerful seminars that combine personal development with leadership strategies.
- **The Leadership Challenge Workshop by Kouzes & Posner** – Based on the book 'The Leadership Challenge,' this workshop helps you apply key leadership principles to real-world situations.
- **Franklin Covey's 7 Habits of Highly Effective People Workshops** – Widely regarded as a top resource for building personal and professional leadership skills.

ONLINE RESOURCES AND PLATFORMS

- **Medium** – A platform with articles from thought leaders on leadership, management, and personal development. Popular leadership publications such as 'The Startup' and 'Better Humans' provide great ideas.
- **MindTools** – A comprehensive online resource offering articles, tools, and courses on leadership and management topics.
- **Harvard Business Review (HBR)** – Provides articles and case studies into leadership and management. HBR's website is a valuable resource for practical, useful advice.
- **TED Talks** – A great platform for short, inspiring talks on innovation and personal growth. Many well-known leaders share their knowledge on TED's stage.
- **Skillshare** – An online platform with a variety of leadership and management courses, focusing on creative and entrepreneurial leadership. Offers hands-on learning with real-world applications.

PODCASTS

- **'The John Maxwell Leadership Podcast'** – John Maxwell, one of the world's foremost leadership experts, shares insightful strategies and advice on becoming a better leader.
- **'The Knowledge Project with Shane Parrish'** – This podcast features interviews with leading thinkers across various fields, exploring decision-making and leadership.
- **'Craig Groeschel Leadership Podcast'** – Offers practical advice on leadership and personal growth, focusing on realistic strategies.
- **'HBR IdeaCast'** – Produced by Harvard Business Review, this podcast covers leadership, management, and business strategies through interviews with top global leaders.
- **'The Leadership Podcast'** – Focuses on leadership strategies and career development often featuring high-profile business leaders and experts.
- **'The Andy Stanley Leadership Podcast'** – Andy Stanley, a renowned pastor and leadership expert, shares practical advice on communication and creating a healthy organisational culture for leaders.
- **'WorkLife with Adam Grant'** – Hosted by organisational psychologist Adam Grant, this podcast delves into the science of work, leadership, and organisational culture, offering fresh perspectives on how to create thriving workplaces.

Staying Ahead in Industry and Technology

For leaders at all levels, I highly recommend that you keep yourself updated in industry and technology.

Industry trends

Foresight is always valuable; it's like the beam headlights of a car when you are driving at night on curvy roads. You want to know what's coming up so that you can take appropriate actions. Industries' change: legislation, processes, technology, best practices, customer habits, and so on. You need to be aware not just of what is around you but also of what is coming ahead.

You can gain this knowledge by reading respected industry media, attending industry conferences and trade shows, and by speaking to or at least following thought leaders in your industry.

Technology

We have been going through enormous changes over the last 50 years and continue to do so, with Artificial Intelligence (AI) as the latest technological revolution. Those who stay ahead with these developments are most likely to keep their jobs.

There are plenty of online platforms you can follow to stay in touch with technology developments. Most of this information will be available from your industry conferences and trade shows but always do your own research.

Why You Must Embrace AI

Artificial Intelligence, or AI, is essentially technology that can carry out tasks that normally require human intelligence. This includes things like learning from data, recognising patterns, making predictions, and even understanding language or images. In other words, AI is the clever part of technology that helps us work more efficiently and solve complex problems faster.

For leaders today, staying on top of AI is not optional; it is vital. AI is reshaping almost every industry:

- **Retail**: Companies like Amazon and Tesco use AI to recommend products, manage stock, and forecast demand.
- **Finance**: Banks rely on AI to detect fraud, assess credit risk, and automate customer support.
- **Healthcare**: AI assists doctors with diagnosing scans, predicting illnesses, and personalising treatment plans.
- **Manufacturing**: AI supports predictive maintenance, quality control, and optimising production lines.
- **Agriculture**: Farmers use AI to forecast crop yields, detect plant disease, and monitor soil conditions.
- **Transport and Logistics**: AI powers route optimisation, traffic management, and autonomous vehicles.
- **Energy**: AI helps predict equipment failures, manage smart grids, and improve efficiency.
- **Marketing and HR**: AI analyses customer behaviour, personalises campaigns, and shortlists candidates efficiently.

Leaders who understand these developments can anticipate trends, identify opportunities, and make smarter strategic decisions. They can guide their teams through change, avoid being caught off guard by new technologies, and keep their organisations competitive. You don't need to be a programmer to benefit. Simply understanding how AI works, what it can and cannot do, and how it affects your sector will allow you to make plan strategically and stay ahead.

Keeping AI knowledge up to date is no longer just an advantage; it is a fundamental part of effective, forward-thinking leadership.

> **Tip**: There are many free AI courses available online from leading universities across the world. One of the popular is Elements of AI, a very accessible massive open online course (MOOC) from the University of Helsinki, which covers the basics of AI, machine learning, neural networks, and the societal impact of AI.

Regular Self-Review Routines

Great leaders don't wait for others to tell them how they're doing; they make reflection a habit. Taking time each week to pause and evaluate your progress, strengths, and setbacks keeps you on track with your leadership goals. Reflect on the challenges you've faced, the decisions you've made, and the lessons you've learned. Every reflection sharpens your judgement and strengthens your confidence.

Is Keeping A Journal or Tracker Necessary?

No, it's not essential. Everyone is different.

If you find it helpful, then it makes sense for you. Documenting ideas, feedback, failures, and successes can reveal patterns over time, highlighting what energises you, what hinders progress, and which behaviours drive results. Journals can transform experience into valuable knowledge and even become the foundation for future mentorship or a leadership memoir.

Chapter 7: Leading International Teams Effectively

When Jürgen Klopp (Manager, Liverpool FC, UK) took charge in 2015, he inherited a squad made up of players from more than a dozen countries. Instead of viewing cultural differences as challenges, he treated them as strengths. By taking time to understand each player's background, showing genuine empathy, and uniting everyone behind a clear vision, 'turning doubters into believers', Klopp built trust and cohesion across borders. His leadership turned Liverpool into one of the most connected and successful international teams in modern football, demonstrating that adaptability and clear communication lie at the centre of global leadership.

Leading international teams requires precisely these qualities. It means recognising and valuing cultural differences, adapting your leadership style, and communicating with clarity across borders. With diverse teams, flexibility, respect for local norms, and alignment with shared goals are essential.

Effective leadership in a global context depends on openness, cultural awareness, and continuous learning, the marks of a truly great international leader.

Understanding Cultural Differences

Understanding cultural diversity is essential when leading international teams. Every culture has its own ways of communicating, working, and making decisions. Recognising these differences helps you avoid misunderstandings and create an inclusive environment. Take the time to learn about your team members' cultural backgrounds, which builds trust and rapport. Table 10 highlights some diverse cultural practices that can guide you.

One approach I use when managing a new team abroad is to arrange a call with a senior team member there and ask them frankly about the cultural norms in that country or region. Don't be shy, it is perfectly acceptable to ask. In my experience, people are often more than happy to explain, and many even take pride in doing so, seeing this gesture as valuable and a mark of respect. Just do it!

Building Cross-Cultural Communication Skills

Effective communication is key when managing a diverse team. It's not just about the words you say, but also about picking up on language nuances, body language, and cultural attitudes towards things like formality and directness.

In some cultures, silence is seen as thoughtful and reflective, while in others, quick and open dialogue is the norm. The trick is to stay flexible and adjust your style to make everyone feel heard and understood. Key point is to respect cultural differences, as this is a very effective way to build stronger connections with teams.

Table 10: Examples of cultural diversity.

Topic	Cultural Practices
Greeting People	Greetings vary widely across cultures. In Japan, bowing shows respect, while in the Middle East, a firm handshake is common, with gender-specific norms. In India, touching the feet of elders is a sign of respect.
Etiquette in Meetings	In Western cultures, meetings are structured and punctual. However, in Latin America or the Middle East, meetings may start later and be more conversational. In some Asian cultures, silence is valued, and prayer times may interrupt business in Muslim-majority countries.
Issues in Business Meetings	In cultures like the US or UK, challenging ideas openly is common, but in Japan or Saudi Arabia, direct confrontation can be seen as disrespectful. Disagreement is usually handled subtly.
Giving Gifts	In Japan or China, gift-giving is an important gesture of respect. In the West, it's less common and can be viewed as inappropriate. In cultures like India or the Middle East, gifts are exchanged during religious festivals like Eid or Diwali.
Timing	In cultures like Germany or the US, punctuality is crucial, while in places like Brazil or India, time is more flexible. Religious observances, such as prayer times in Muslim countries, can also affect scheduling.
Food in Offices	In the US or UK, employees often eat at their desks, while in Spain or Italy, meals are more social. In Muslim-majority countries, halal food is common, and in Hindu-majority workplaces, vegetarian food is preferred.
Religious Practices	Religious practices affect work life: prayer times in Muslim countries, festivals like Diwali in India, and holidays such as Christmas and Easter in Christian cultures.

Be mindful that gestures and behaviours can have different meanings across cultures. For example, the 'OK' sign is fine in Europe and North America but offensive in Brazil. Shaking hands with Muslim women in some Middle Eastern countries is discouraged unless they initiate it, while in Japan, bowing may be preferred. Small actions like this shape how professionalism and respect are perceived.

Adapting Leadership Styles for Different Cultures – Is This Possible?

Textbooks advise adjusting leadership for different cultures, but it depends. When relocating, adapting to local practices builds trust. For remote teams across regions, fully changing your style is unrealistic. Be sensitive to cultural differences, encourage mutual adaptation, and focus on understanding. Good leadership is about flexibility and respect, not total transformation.

Here is a summary of different leadership styles:

- Western cultures (USA, Canada, UK, Australia) generally favour democratic and participative leadership styles, encouraging collaboration, input from team members, and promoting innovation.
- Asian cultures (China, Japan, South Korea, Malaysia, Indonesia, Russia) often prioritise authoritarian or hierarchical leadership, focusing on seniority, authority, and group harmony.

- Middle Eastern countries (Saudi Arabia, UAE, Qatar, North Africa, Iran) often feature authoritarian leadership combined with charismatic qualities, where leaders hold significant control and inspire loyalty.

- African countries (Nigeria, Kenya, South Africa, Ghana, Uganda) leadership often blends hierarchy with participative elements. Respect for seniority, community engagement, personal relationships, and charisma are key to influence and effectiveness.

- Latin American countries (Brazil, Argentina, Mexico) blend charismatic and paternalistic leadership styles, where personal relationships and loyalty are important.

- South Asian countries (India, Pakistan, Bangladesh) display a mix of paternalistic and authoritarian leadership styles, with a focus on authority and loyalty, but also an increasing trend towards transformational leadership in some cases.

Effective Communication Across Borders

Speak Plainly to Ensure Everyone on a Global Team Understands

Effective communication is essential in international teams. You need to overcome language barriers, time zone differences, and cultural nuances. Make your communication clear, direct, and respectful to ensure everyone is on the same page. Avoid jargon, idioms, and overly complex language. For example, terms like 'circle back', 'low-hanging fruit', or 'bandwidth' can confuse non-native speakers, as can idioms like 'hit the ground running' or 'think outside the box'. Always clarify points that might cause confusion to ensure understanding across cultures.

Case Study: D&G's Marketing Missteps in China: How to Balance Fashion Brand Strategy and Cultural Sensitivity?

In 2018, D&G launched an advertising campaign featuring a Chinese model struggling to eat Italian food with chopsticks, intending to highlight the fusion of Italian and Chinese cultures. However, the ad was widely seen as racist and culturally insensitive, perpetuating stereotypes and mocking Chinese traditions. The backlash from Chinese consumers was immediate and severe, resulting in the cancellation of the brand's major fashion show in Shanghai, removal of products from Chinese e-commerce platforms, and lasting damage to D&G's reputation and sales in China.

Source: *Harvard Business Review*

Learn To Greet in Local Languages

My experience is that taking the time to greet colleagues in their own language can transform perceptions and help your team gel faster. It shows respect, cultural awareness, and a willingness to connect personally, which builds trust and camaraderie. Even a simple 'hello' in someone's native tongue can make a lasting positive impression. Table 11 shows greetings in popular languages that you can use.

Improving Your Team's Business Language

A highly effective strategy I use with international teams is helping members improve their business language skills, so they feel more comfortable and confident communicating with me. Without this, people often stay quiet, which can hinder collaboration and innovation. While English is the *de facto* international business language, many team members around the world are still developing proficiency. Offering business English courses as part of their professional development not only boosts skills but also creates a positive, motivated, and happier team.

Table 11: Global greetings for your team.

Language	Greeting	Transliteration	Meaning
Arabic	السلام عليكم	As-salāmu ʿalaykum	Peace be upon you
Bengali	السلام عليكم or স্যালো	As-salāmu ʿalaykum; Hyālō	Peace be upon you; Hello
English	Hello	Hello	Standard greeting
Filipino / Tagalog	Kamusta	Kah-moo-sta	How are you? / Hello
French	Bonjour	bon-ZHOOR	Good day
German	Guten Tag	GOO-ten tahg	Good day
Greek	Γειά σας	Yia sas	Hello (formal)
Hausa	Sannu	SAH-noo	Hello
Hindi	नमस्ते	Namaste	I bow to you / Hello
Indonesian / Malay	السلام عليكم or Halo	As-salāmu ʿalaykum; Halo	Peace be upon you; Hello
Italian	Ciao	CHOW	Hello / Hi

Japanese	こんにちは	Konnichiwa	Good afternoon / Hello
Korean	안녕하세요	Annyeong haseyo	Hello (polite)
Mandarin Chinese	你好	Nǐ hǎo	Hello / Hi
Persian / Farsi	سلام	Salam	Hello
Portuguese	Olá	oh-LAH	Hello
Punjabi	ਸਤ ਸ੍ਰੀ ਅਕਾਲ	Sat Sri Akal	Hello (Sikh greeting)
Russian	Здравствуйте	Zdravstvuyte	Hello (formal)
Spanish	Hola	OH-lah	Hello
Swahili	Jambo	JAHM-bo	Hello / How are you?
Thai	สวัสดี	Sà-wàt-dee	Hello
Turkish	Merhaba	MEHR-ha-bah	Hello
Urdu	السلام علیکم or بیلو	As-salāmu ʿalaykum; Hello	Peace be upon you; Hello
Yoruba	Bawo	BAH-woh	Hello
Zulu	Sawubona	sah-woo-BOH-nah	Hello

Adapting to Different Work Habits

In an international team, each member may have a different approach to work, from problem-solving to decision-making. Be flexible with your expectations and leadership style to accommodate these differences. Encourage teamwork and ensure everyone's voice is heard and respected.

For example, working hours and daily routines vary globally:

- **Spain:** Long lunch breaks, typically 2–3 hours, are common, and the workday may extend into the evening.
- **Germany:** Punctuality is highly valued, and lunch breaks are usually short, around 30–45 minutes.
- **Japan:** Employees often stay late at the office as a sign of dedication.
- **United States:** Standard office hours are typically 9 am–5 pm, with shorter lunch breaks.
- **Middle East:** The workweek may run Sunday to Thursday, and prayer times or cultural observances influence daily schedules.
- **Nordic countries:** Emphasis on work-life balance, with flexible hours and early finishes.

Being aware of these differences allows you to coordinate meetings, set deadlines, and manage expectations effectively across your team.

Empathy as a Leadership Tool

Empathy is a vital leadership skill when managing diverse teams. Understanding and validating your team members' perspectives helps build stronger connections and promotes better collaboration. Show genuine care for their well-being and professional development, which can lead to higher engagement and productivity.

"I walk in their shoes to understand."

Different team members have different personal and cultural needs that leaders should recognise. For example:

- In many Muslim-majority countries, employees may need flexible working arrangements to care for elderly parents or attend religious obligations such as Friday prayers.

- Attending funerals or observing mourning periods is very important in cultures across South Asia, the Middle East, and Latin America, and may require temporary leave or schedule adjustments.

- In Japan and other East Asian cultures, employees may prioritise family obligations such as caring for children or ageing relatives and may value clear expectations around work-life balance.

- Western cultures may place emphasis on mental health days or flexible hours for personal development and well-being.

Leaders who show genuine sensitivity and adapt thoughtfully to their team's diverse needs are the ones most likely to achieve lasting success.

In addition to empathy, I would strongly argue that cultural intelligence is equally important for leaders. So, what is cultural intelligence? It's the ability to adapt leadership styles to the unique cultural contexts of teams. Recent research shows that leaders with high cultural intelligence understand and respond to cultural norms and needs, leading to better collaboration and improved team performance.[7]

---

[7] Ang, S., & Van Dyne, L. (2008). *Handbook of Cultural Intelligence: Theory, Measurement, and Applications.* M.E. Sharpe.

Appendix A – Useful Frameworks for Leaders

Table 12: Useful frameworks for new leaders.

Chapter Heading	Frameworks / Purpose & Use
Chapter 1: Understanding The Foundation of Leading People	• Blake & Mouton Managerial Grid – maps leadership style based on concern for people vs. concern for results. • Hersey & Blanchard Situational Leadership – adapts leadership approach based on team readiness and competence. • Leadership Pipeline Model – outlines leadership growth stages and required competencies. • Transformational Leadership Model – Focuses on inspiring and motivating teams to exceed expectations by fostering an environment of trust, empowerment, and shared vision.
Chapter 2: Establishing Core Values in Leadership Practice	• Kouzes & Posner Five Practices of Exemplary Leadership – guides leaders in modeling values, inspiring vision, and encouraging others. • Servant Leadership Model – emphasizes prioritizing team needs, humility, and ethical behavior.

Chapter 3: A Leadership Integration Plan	• Values-Based Leadership Framework – aligns decisions and behaviors with personal and organisational values. • SMART Goals Framework – sets specific, measurable, achievable, relevant, and time-bound objectives. • OKRs (Objectives and Key Results) – aligns team objectives with organisational priorities. • Eisenhower Matrix / Time Management Grid – prioritizes tasks based on urgency and importance.
30-Day Plan for New Team Leaders	• 30-60-90 Day Plan Template – structures early leadership actions, priorities, and milestones. • SWOT Analysis (Team Member Focus) – identifies individual strengths, weaknesses, opportunities, and threats. • Stakeholder Mapping – visualizes influence, interest, and relationships within the team and organisation. • The GROW Model – A coaching tool that stands for Goal, Reality, Options, and Will, which can help new leaders facilitate constructive conversations with team members about their development and performance.
60-Day Plan for Supervisors & Managers	• 9-Box Talent Matrix – Evaluates team performance vs. potential, helping with development planning and identifying future leaders.

	• Competency Framework – Assesses the skills required for roles and highlights any gaps in capabilities. • RACI Matrix – Clarifies roles and responsibilities across projects or processes, ensuring everyone knows their responsibilities. • 360-Degree Feedback – Gathers comprehensive feedback from peers, subordinates, and supervisors to assess leadership effectiveness and identify areas for growth. • Performance Review Framework – Structures regular evaluations to track individual and team progress, aligning performance with organisational goals. • Team Development Stages (Tuckman's Model) – Guides managers through the stages of team development (Forming, Storming, Norming, Performing, Adjourning), helping to recognise and address team dynamics at each stage.
Chapter 4: Getting to Know Your Team and Key Stakeholders	• Team SWOT Analysis – captures individual strengths, weaknesses, opportunities, and risks. • 360-Degree Feedback – gathers input from peers, subordinates, and managers. • Social Network / Influence Mapping – identifies key stakeholders and relationships.
Chapter 5: Setting Direction and	• OKRs – aligns team goals with organisational priorities.

Establishing Early Wins	• KPI Dashboards – tracks progress and early wins. • Gantt Charts / Project Planning Tools – structures timelines for objectives and quick wins.
Chapter 6: Driving Team Performance and Continuous Growth	• Performance Appraisal Matrix – evaluates team members across competencies. • Coaching and Feedback Models (e.g., GROW Model) – supports development and problem-solving. • Continuous Improvement Frameworks (Kaizen, P organisational DCA Cycle) – fosters ongoing team growth. • Recognition & Reward Models – reinforces desired behaviors and accountability.
Chapter 7: Leading International Teams Effectively	• Hofstede's Cultural Dimensions – guides leaders on cross-cultural differences. • Globe Study Leadership Dimensions – compares leadership expectations across cultures. • Adaptive Leadership Framework – adjusts style to different cultural and organisational contexts. • Intercultural Communication Models – improves collaboration and understanding across borders.

Other Titles and Services from the Publisher

Selling in the Middle East

A practical guide for sales professionals

A practical guide designed to help sales professionals and organisations navigate this complex yet rewarding landscape. The book provides essential insights into the region's cultural nuances, business practices, and sales strategies.

Evolution of Sales Methodologies

Explore how sales practices have evolved over time

This book explores the evolution of sales strategies, from ancient barter systems to modern practices like BANT and Challenger Selling. It examines historical shifts and impacts of digital tools, CRM systems, and AI on the sales landscape.

Scan the QR code to visit the website, or go to: oxfordhousemedia.com

Leadership Coaching Services

Great leaders aren't born; they're developed.

We specialise in leadership coaching and personal profile enhancement, helping you build confidence, refine your skills, and strengthen your presence to make a lasting impact.

Scan the QR code to visit the website, or go to:
inspiredmanager.com/coaching

Inspired by this book?
Please leave an online review – we'd really appreciate it!